THE NORTON SERIES ON
SOCIAL EMOTIONAL LEARNING SOLUTIONS
PATRICIA A. JENNINGS, SERIES EDITOR

*Mindfulness in the Secondary Classroom: A Guide for
Teaching Adolescents*
Patricia C. Broderick

*SEL Every Day: Integrating Social and Emotional Learning
with Instruction in Secondary Classrooms*
Meena Srinivasan

*Assessing Students' Social and Emotional Learning:
A Guide to Meaningful Measurement*
Clark McKown

*Mindfulness in the PreK–5 Classroom:
Helping Students Stress Less and Learn More*
Patricia A. Jennings

*Preventing Bullying in Schools:
A Social and Emotional Learning Approach to Early Intervention*
Catherine P. Bradshaw and Tracy Evian Waasdorp

NORTON BOOKS IN EDUCATION

Advance Praise

"Meena Srinivasan offers educators an invaluable resource for implementing SEL in their schools and classrooms. Drawing on her own experiences as a teacher and a leader, Srinivasan offers insights and suggestions that are grounded, actionable, wise, and potentially transformational."

—Elena Aguilar, Founder and President of Bright Morning Consulting, author of *The Art of Coaching*, *The Art of Coaching Teams*, and *Onward: Cultivating Emotional Resilience in Educators*

"Meena Srinivasan offers educators, parents, and students an important and timely book. Grounded in the recognition that cognition and emotion are inextricably linked, *SEL Every Day* presents both the research underpinnings and the practical actions that schools and teachers can take to develop students' social-emotional capacities. Let me get personal: I have two young granddaughters and I most definitely want them to be with teachers who practice SEL—every day!"

—Jay McTighe, M.Ed., educational author and consultant, co-author of the *Understanding by Design®* series

"I could not put this book down! From Meena Srinivasan's *SEL Every Day: Integrating Social and Emotional Learning with Instruction in Secondary Classrooms*, I learned numerous practices and strategies to integrate SEL with Common Core, as well as how to create learning environments where everyone thrives. SEL self-assessments, lesson planning templates, community circle guidelines, mindfulness practices, and reflective questions are provided, making it easy to integrate SEL into subject matter instruction! An exceptional resource for teachers!"

—Wendy Baron, M.A., Co-Founder, New Teacher Center, Chief Officer, Social and Emotional Learning, Emerita

"*SEL Every Day* is the book that the field of secondary school SEL has been waiting for. It needs to be in the hands of every secondary school teacher who cares about teaching the whole child and knows that both teaching and learning are intrinsically social and emotional. Through Srinivasan's own embodiment of SEL practices and her direct and extensive firsthand work with students and teachers, this book puts to rest the myth that the teaching and learning of SEL is separate and too time-consuming for the secondary classroom."

—Linda Lantieri, Author, *Building Emotional Intelligence*, Senior Program Advisor, *Collaborative for Academic, Social, and Emotional Learning* (CASEL)

"*SEL Every Day* masterfully addresses secondary school educators' biggest challenges around SEL: how to fit SEL into the curriculum without taking time away from academic content and how to teach it in a developmentally-appropriate way that meets adolescents' needs. But Srinivasan takes these challenges one step further and centers them in a pedagogy of love—'the ultimate goal of SEL'—where both the adults and their students 'feel seen, safe, appreciated, and loved.'"

—Vicki Zakrzewski, Ph.D., Education Director, Greater Good Science Center at UC Berkeley

"Educators, students, and parents alike are calling for more attention to social and emotional learning in our schools and communities. This book paints a compelling picture of both the challenges and the urgency of ensuring our adolescent students experience SEL in their schools and classrooms every day. Srinivasan brings rich knowledge of SEL research and lived experience leading and teaching SEL to this practical and inspiring guide to integrating SEL into our secondary classrooms."

—Karen Van Ausdal, Senior Director of Practice with CASEL

"*SEL Every Day* is a remarkable map for guiding educators to integrate SEL into their secondary educational settings. Meena Srinivasan is one of the few experts who has done the real work of implementing SEL on a systems level, while embodying and modeling the true principals of mindfulness and SEL from the inside out. This book is full of practical, scientific, and strategic methods for cultivating a more compassionate school environment. *SEL Every Day* is accessible, full of relatable stories, and a delight to read."

—Daniel Rechtschaffen, MFT, author of *The Way of Mindful Education* and *The Mindful Education Workbook*

SEL Every Day

Integrating Social and Emotional Learning With Instruction in Secondary Classrooms

MEENA SRINIVASAN

W. W. Norton & Company

Independent Publishers Since 1923

New York London

For information about permission to reproduce selections from this book, write to Permissions, W. W. Norton & Company, Inc., 500 Fifth Avenue, New York, NY 10110

For information about special discounts for bulk purchases, please contact W. W. Norton Special Sales at specialsales@wwnorton.com or 800-233-4830

Manufacturing by Versa Press
Book design by Molly Heron
Production manager: Katelyn MacKenzie

ISBN: 978-0-393-71359-6 (pbk.)

W. W. Norton & Company, Inc., 500 Fifth Avenue, New York, N.Y. 10110
www.wwnorton.com

W. W. Norton & Company Ltd., 15 Carlisle Street, London W1D 3BS

1 2 3 4 5 6 7 8 9 0

For my son Kailash and the next generation. May SEL help create thriving, resilient, courageous, and caring young people as we build a more compassionate, equitable, and WOKE world together.

Contents

From the Series Editor

The SOCIAL AND EMOTIONAL LEARNING SOLUTIONS (SEL SOLU-
TIONS) SERIES features compact books for educators focused on recommended SEL practices from experts in the field. Cutting-edge research
continues to confirm that teaching students social and emotional skills pays
off in improved behavior and academic learning that continues into adulthood as success in life. The books are intended to provide school leaders
and classroom teachers with SEL tools and strategies that are grounded in
research yet highly accessible, so readers can confidently begin using them
to transform school culture, improve student behavior, and foster learning
with the proven benefits of SEL.

It is with great enthusiasm that I introduce Meena Srinivasan's new
book *SEL Every Day: Integrating Social and Emotional Learning With Instruction in Secondary Classrooms*. This much needed volume is a treasure for
educators looking for research-based approaches to support adolescents'

social and emotional learning. The need for such a book became blatantly obvious to me when my son became an adolescent and a dramatic change came over him. From my perspective, it seemed like he was regressing in his social and emotional skills. Overly irritable and touchy, he seemed less empathetic than he had been as a younger child. I wondered, "Where did my kind, sweet boy go?" Like many parents, I wasn't sure how best to help him. But we now have a much better understanding of the dramatic developmental transformations that adolescence involves, how these changes impact children's social and emotional development, and how to provide the support they need. This book fills a critical need; there are many resources for elementary-level educators but few for those in middle and high schools.

As children enter puberty, they are flooded by hormones that their bodies are not used to and their brains go through important changes, with different regions of the brain developing at different rates. At this stage of development the limbic system, where emotions are processed, develops more quickly than the prefrontal cortex (PFC), where executive functions are based. Executive functions allow the individual to differentiate among conflicting thoughts, make judgements about good and bad, determine the future consequences of current activities, engage in goal-directed behavior, and exercise social "control," which is the ability to inhibit urges that might result in socially unacceptable behavior. The developmental imbalance during adolescence, when the limbic system is ahead of the PFC, results in teens' active engagement in social media, parties, gossip, sex, substance use, and other behaviors that provide stimulation. However, some of these activities are dangerous and as we all know, adolescents often make unwise decisions.

Contrary to the common misconception that adolescents don't need SEL—that teens should have learned these skills already—these developmental changes make adolescence an optimal time to teach SEL. We know that the brain is more malleable during this time, which gives us a critical window of opportunity to promote self-understanding, self-control, and better decision-making. The teen brain is also more vulnerable to stress, making this an optimal time to learn stress reduction and self-care skills such as mindful awareness practices. SEL is a lifelong learning journey and at every age we can learn new skills and adapt to new challenges. The dramatic changes during adolescence provide both a window of opportunity and a necessity to support social and emotional development.

Based in the most current research on adolescent social and emotional development, *SEL Every Day* is an accessible guide for teachers about how to integrate SEL into their instruction. Meena Srinivasan offers a holistic approach to SEL and academic instruction, rather than treating it as a stand-alone "add-on" or intervention. This approach frees time by efficiently embedding SEL into existing teaching practices. The book also provides easy-to-use strategies for promoting a positive school culture by building strong teacher-student and peer relationships, using approaches that are based in equity and cultural responsiveness. Each chapter begins with a story about how the SEL concepts presented in the chapter have been applied by an educator. Other highlights include notes from the field that clearly demonstrate how things work on the ground. In addition, the text explores the connections between SEL and the Common Core, project-based learning, personalized learning, and college and career readiness. I am confident that *SEL Every Day* will become your go-to resource for SEL instruction.

Patricia A. Jennings, M.Ed., Ph.D.
Editor, Norton Series on Social and Emotional Learning Solutions

Acknowledgments

Countless individuals played a role in bringing this book into being. I want to especially acknowledge my SEL teammates in the Oakland Unified School District (OUSD), Sonny Kim and Mary Hurley, and our beloved CASEL consultants, my adopted aunties, Chris Hiroshima and Ann McKay Bryson. For the past 6 years we have been on a journey together on how to implement SEL in a system as complex as a large, urban public school district and we have learned so much from and with the teachers, leaders, students, staff, and parents in the OUSD community. Heartfelt appreciation to my long-time mentor and dear friend, CASEL co-founder, Linda Lantieri, for always believing in me and being my very own "SEL fairy god mother" all these years. Many thanks to Carol Collins and the team at Norton for their guidance and support in this publication and to Tish Jennings for inviting me to contribute to the SEL Solutions Series.

Deep gratitude to my parents, who are the most loving, supportive, and generous people I know—they moved out to Richmond, California, 6 days after the birth of my son to help me out so I could actually write this book. And of course, much thanks goes to my loving husband, Chihiro Wimbush, for his unwavering support in all of my professional endeavors and my baby boy, Kailash, for his gorgeous smiles and sweet demeanor, giving me the daily inspiration needed to write this book.

Finally, I'd like to thank the NoVo Foundation for their financial commitment to advancing the field of social and emotional learning (SEL). I'm very grateful to be a NoVo grantee, their approach to SEL serves as a continual reminder of why I do what I do.

"NoVo believes that SEL, brought to scale, can and will play a significant role in shifting our culture of systemic inequality and violence toward a new ethos that values and prioritizes collaboration and partnership . . . We believe, based on strong social science evidence, that SEL has particular power to unlock a broad range of human capacities—intellectual and emotional—which prepare children to co-create a kinder, more interconnected, and equitable future."

SEL Every Day

SEL in the Secondary Context: Why SEL Is Critical for Adolescents

Any teacher who thinks that SEL should be done in younger grades is 100% right. We 100% wish that all of our students came fully equipped with all the social and emotional intelligence and skills and attributes that we would want everyone to come with. Sadly and unfortunately, that's not our reality. This is something that a lot of our young people don't come to school equipped with, and just like we do with any young person that needs support in learning, whether it be algebra or English, we take the time to slow down and develop those skills so they can learn to be successful. SEL is no different. We have an equal responsibility to slow down and take time to find ways to meaningfully incorporate SEL into our teaching.
—Matin Abdel-Qawi, principal, Oakland High School, Oakland, California

"Social and emotional learning (SEL) is the process by which children, adolescents, and adults can acquire and apply the necessary knowledge and skills to understand and manage their emotions, feel and express empathy for others, set and achieve positive goals, and make responsible decisions" (CASEL). SEL skills are fundamental for effectiveness in life and are especially valuable during the emotionally turbulent years of adolescence. Despite recognizing its value, middle and high schools do not always make room to offer a standalone SEL program, and administrators and teachers often state that they don't have time to implement SEL.

It is common in some school communities to view social and emotional learning as separate from academics and instruction, and there is insufficient evidence that solely skills-based SEL programs provide the most effective approach for teenagers (Yeager, 2017). This book is for middle and high school leaders and teachers who understand the need for SEL as an integrated part of instruction rather than just a stand-alone SEL program. It will help teachers see how SEL is in fact not separate from academics or instruction, but is integral to and interdependent with quality teaching and learning. *SEL Every Day: Integrating Social and Emotional Learning With Instruction in Secondary Classrooms* draws upon the latest research and resources on SEL-integrated instruction and offers an accessible guide for educators on how to begin to incorporate SEL into their everyday teaching.

While there are a number of research-based strategies and evidence-based programs for implementing SEL in elementary classrooms, there are far fewer resources and less guidance around how to implement SEL in middle and high school settings. Prioritizing SEL can be challenging for secondary school teachers for a number of reasons:

- Middle and high school teachers have far less time for interaction with individual students compared to their elementary school counterparts.

- Secondary-level classes tend to be more content driven.
- There's a misconception that by middle school, students should come already equipped with basic SEL skills.

These factors, combined with the pressures of college and career readiness, leave little room for SEL instruction. However, given the current nature and structure of secondary schools, it's critical that teachers find ways to infuse SEL across academic content and ensure that it becomes foundational to their teaching practice.

The majority of teachers believe that SEL improves college preparation and workforce readiness, yet only a minority are engaged in schoolwide SEL (Civic Enterprises, Bridgeland, Bruce, & Hariharan, 2013). This book aims to be a resource in bridging the disconnect between what teachers feel will benefit students and what's actually being taught. Approaching SEL and academic instruction as one "holistic package—rather than treating it as an additional, siloed initiative with separate offices and stand-alone interventions—can streamline and strengthen the work of teachers, principals, and district leaders" (Johnson & Wiener, 2017).

My Story

At the time of writing this book, I'm experiencing the confluence of the three most critical stages of rapid development in one's life—early childhood, adolescence, and matrescence. I became a mother for the first time just as I embarked on writing the first draft of this book. Similar to adolescence, matrescence is the developmental phase of new motherhood when hormones surge, bodies morph, and identity and relationships shift (Sacks, 2017). Going through my own experience of incredible physical and emotional changes while watching my newborn son, Kailash, transform daily, has reminded me of the intensity of adolescence and helped me empathize even more deeply with my middle and high school students, whose bodies are also undergoing tremendous growth and development. It is so important for us as educators to create compassionate, understanding, and safe containers for learning, especially during adolescence.

Writing this book has been a deeply personal experience for me. I firmly believe that SEL is the vehicle for creating a more compassionate and equitable world, and in my 16 years as an educator, I've seen firsthand how prioritizing SEL can be transformational for students, teachers, families, schools, and entire districts.

I taught middle and high school for over a decade in a variety of settings (public, private, urban, and international schools) where mindfulness and SEL were fundamental to teaching and learning. As people who were inspired to become educators, we probably all have had the experience of being taught by an extraordinary teacher—perhaps more than a few. What were the qualities they had that allowed you, the student, to excel? Most likely they had a high degree of social and emotional intelligence that helped you feel seen, safe, and appreciated in the classroom. Several years ago, well before mindfulness became a buzzword, I had the profound opportunity to study mindfulness with some of the world's best-known teachers, and growing my own personal practice brought a sense of peace and deep meaning to my life. Cultivating present-moment awareness enabled me to better understand my students, resulting in stronger relationships and more effective teaching. My journey as a mindful educator and the resources and practices I engaged in and developed while in the classroom culminated in the publication of *Teach, Breathe, Learn: Mindfulness in and out of the Classroom* (Srinivasan, 2014). *Teach, Breathe, Learn* was one of the first education resources published to make mindfulness accessible to educators worldwide.

Around the time of *Teach, Breathe, Learn*'s publication, one of my mentors, Collaborative for Academic, Social, and Emotional Learning (CASEL)[*] cofounder Linda Lantieri, urged me to transition out of the classroom and join an innovative team in the Oakland Unified School District working in partnership with CASEL to implement SEL system-wide in the school district. Oakland, along with 10 other large, complex, urban school districts in the United States, was part of the Collaborating Districts Initiative (CDI), an effort to study and scale high-quality, evidence-based academic, social, and emotional learning. Thanks to generous funding from the NoVo Foundation, the goal of this initiative was to help superintendents and school districts move beyond test scores and prioritize whole-child education while also creating resources and tools that could then be used to support large-scale SEL implementation in other districts. Being part of the CDI learning

---

[*] CASEL is the world's leading organization for advancing research, policy, and practice in the field of SEL.

community has been a tremendous opportunity to learn from, and with, other districts engaged in similar work. One of my focus areas on our SEL team was middle and high school, and what I quickly discovered through my conversations with my counterparts in other districts was a tremendous gap in SEL resources available for middle and high school teachers, particularly related to SEL-integrated instruction, which is why I decided to write this book.

It is important to note that the optimal approach to schoolwide SEL implementation is systemic. In fact, developmental psychologist Stephanie Jones and her research team at the Harvard Graduate School of Education spent 5 years studying the effectiveness of SEL programs, and their findings showed that successful approaches to SEL employ a whole-school approach involving all adults in the building (not just teachers) being trained in a common set of practices and language. This is especially important during the times when students have less structure (in hallways, at lunchtime, on the bus, etc.) (Shafer, 2016).

Unfortunately, not every school has the time, resources, capacity, or conditions to implement SEL in this way from the start. This book can be used either as a resource in a CASEL-developed systemic approach that also involves SEL curriculum and instruction, schoolwide practices and policies, and family and community partnerships, or as a starting point for individual teachers or teaching teams who wish to fine-tune their teaching practices to infuse and integrate SEL and make it more explicit in their instruction.

GOING DEEPER

Transformative Educational Leadership (TEL) is an empowering, racially and culturally diverse, compassion-centered, innovative program for educational leaders who are called to integrate mindfulness-based social, emotional, academic and ethical learning into schools and school systems. TEL fills an important gap as the only training program dedicated exclusively to building leadership capacity in service of systemic SEL implementation. Learn more at: https://www.teleadership.org/

What Is SEL?

With the passage of the Every Student Succeeds Act in 2015, states now have more flexibility in how they measure student achievement. The law replaced references to "core academic subjects" and instead called for a "well-rounded education" for all students, thus raising the profile of SEL in education (Rosales, 2017). This coincides with advances in research in the fields of neuroscience and education that demonstrates how social and emotional development is not only central to learning but critical in order to thrive in all aspects of life—students' careers, relationships, and their overall health and well-being.

So, what is SEL? It's a term that is now widely used but often without defining what it really means. In fact, in a 2017 analysis of the SEL field conducted by Education First, creating coherence across SEL frameworks and terminologies was named as a top priority. The National Commission on Social, Emotional, and Academic Development at the Aspen Institute is trying to fill this gap by bringing together policy makers, practitioners, and researchers from across the field. In May 2018 they offered the following comprehensive definition:

> Social and emotional development comprises specific skills and competencies that people need in order to set goals, manage behavior, build relationships, and process and remember information. These skills and competencies develop in a complex system of contexts, interactions, and relationships, suggesting that organizations must take a comprehensive approach to promoting social and emotional development—addressing adult skills and beliefs; organizational culture, climate, and norms; and routines and structures that guide basic interactions and instruction—and that such approaches are most effective when designed to match the needs and contexts of specific organizations and communities. Put simply, social and emotional development is not just about the skills that students and adults possess and deploy; it is also about the features of the educational setting itself, including culture and climate. (Aspen Institute, 2018)

This definition takes into account the importance of context when engaging in SEL and positions SEL as more than just a set of skills and competencies developed irrespective of culture and community—or as something only for young people. One of the most important aspects of this definition is the emphasis on addressing adult skills and beliefs. Central to the success of SEL is an examination of adult beliefs. SEL is not about fixing students but rather about seeing the whole picture of who we are, especially our strengths and assets.

In Oakland, we developed SEL standards, but unlike most other districts we specifically designated our standards to be pre-K–adult, signaling that SEL is equally important for adults. Early on in my career, a former district leader seemed to contend that teachers either have SEL skills or don't. He seemed to believe that these skills were innate. From my experience working with students, adults, and my own personal SEL journey, I know that these skills can be taught and learned. Moreover, studies that say "social, emotional, and cognitive skills are not predetermined by one's genetic blueprint; our genes interact with experience so that these skills emerge, grow, and change over time" (Jones & Kahn, 2017) back up the notion that we can all develop more emotional intelligence with practice, given the right conditions.

There are also significant studies showing that when teachers prioritize SEL there is more effective classroom management, and when teachers grow a personal SEL practice they experience less stress and burnout, so focusing on SEL is a win-win for both students and teachers. In fact, a cost-benefit study of SEL interventions showed a positive return on investment averaging a yield of $11 in long-term benefits for every $1 invested (Jones

& Kahn, 2017); a 20-year study shows a link between SEL instruction in kindergarten and well-being in early adulthood (RWJF, 2015); and a 2011 meta-analysis found an 11 percentile-point gain in academic achievement (Durlak, Weissberg, Dymnicki, Taylor, & Schellinger).

SEL Framework

While I encourage you to engage your school community in defining SEL for your context, when initially communicating with colleagues, parents, and students about SEL, the following definition from CASEL may be more accessible.

> Social and emotional learning (SEL) is the process through which children and adults acquire and effectively apply the knowledge, attitudes, and skills necessary to understand and manage emotions, set and achieve positive goals, feel and show empathy for others, establish and maintain positive relationships, and make responsible decisions.

CASEL's Framework for Systemic SEL identifies five interdependent core competencies that I use as a way to engage with SEL in this book.

FIGURE 1.1: Framework for Systemic Social and Emotional Learning
Collaborative for Academic, Social, and Emotional Learning (© CASEL)

Self-awareness

The ability to accurately recognize one's own emotions, thoughts, and values and how they influence behavior. The ability to accurately assess one's strengths and limitations, with a well-grounded sense of confidence, optimism, and a "growth mind-set."

- Identifying emotions
- Accurate self-perception
- Recognizing strengths
- Self-confidence
- Self-efficacy

Self-management

The ability to successfully regulate one's emotions, thoughts, and behaviors in different situations—effectively managing stress, controlling impulses, and motivating oneself. The ability to set and work toward personal and academic goals.

- Impulse control
- Stress management
- Self-discipline
- Self-motivation
- Goal-setting
- Organizational skills

Social awareness

The ability to take the perspective of and empathize with others, including those from diverse backgrounds and cultures. The ability to understand social and ethical norms for behavior and to recognize family, school, and community resources and supports.

- Perspective-taking
- Empathy
- Appreciating diversity
- Respect for others

Relationship skills

The ability to establish and maintain healthy and rewarding relationships with diverse individuals and groups. The ability to communicate clearly, listen well, cooperate with others, resist inappropriate social pressure, negotiate conflict constructively, and seek and offer help when needed.

- Communication
- Social engagement
- Relationship-building
- Teamwork

Responsible decision-making

The ability to make constructive choices about personal behavior and social interactions based on ethical standards, safety concerns, and social norms. The realistic evaluation of consequences of various actions, and a consideration of the well-being of oneself and others.

- Identifying problems
- Analyzing situations
- Solving problems
- Evaluating
- Reflecting
- Ethical responsibility

(www.casel.org)

Developmentally Appropriate SEL Indicators

Many districts and several states have created developmentally appropriate SEL indicators using the CASEL framework as a guide. This is also a growing area of focus for SEL researchers as we continue to deepen our understanding of developmentally appropriate SEL and its performance descriptors. While I encourage you to engage your community in building out these indicators for your context, you can look to other states and districts as a guide and modify based on your context. These resources are public and freely available. For example, the Illinois State Board of Education has SEL standards and performance descriptors for each grade level K–12.

Collaborating States Initiative to Advance SEL

Even if your school or district doesn't yet have SEL standards, if you live in the United States you can see if your state has developed them and use these standards as a guide and rationale for prioritizing SEL in your classroom. In 2003, CASEL was part of the working group that developed the Illinois SEL standards. These were the nation's first state-sponsored K–12 standards for SEL. During the next 12 years, CASEL partnered with eight additional state working groups to advance their SEL initiatives. In 2016, CASEL's Collaborating States Initiative (CSI) was formally launched, and there are now 25 state education agencies working on policies to help implement SEL in their respective states (Dusenbury & Weissberg, 2018). Similar to the CDI I participated in, the CSI is also a community of practice learning from and with each other as they advance SEL in their states.

Adult SEL

We don't have to wait until we have our own SEL down before we share it with our students, because SEL is a lifelong process. A great way of understanding this is an analogy offered by one of my mentors, CASEL SEL professional development consultant Ann McKay Bryson. Ann invites us to think about the interplay between adult SEL and the ways we engage young people in SEL as the two pedals on a bicycle. Each pedal is equally important, and they work together to multiply the effects of our effort, reinforcing each other as they move us forward.

GOING DEEPER

1. *Onward: Cultivating Emotional Resilience in Educators* (2018) is a beautiful book written by my former Oakland Unified School District colleague, Elena Aguilar. This book is a useful resource for building our own Adult SEL competencies while also tackling the challenge of educator stress through providing a practical framework for taking the burnout out of teaching.

2. The Greater Good Science Center at UC Berkeley has developed a number of exceptional resources to support the development of Adult SEL competencies. They also host a week long annual Summer Institute for Educators focused on educator well-being and personal growth through integrating the science of social-emotional learning, mindfulness, and other areas of prosocial human development. I had the honor of serving as guest faculty a few summers ago and I saw first-hand the powerful experiences participants have. Learn more at: https://ggsc.berkeley.edu/who_we_serve/educators.

Transformative SEL and Educational Equity

The paradox of education is precisely this—that as one begins to become conscious one begins to examine the society in which [they are] being educated.

—James Baldwin

In Oakland, we've expanded the CASEL definition of social and emotional learning to also include an equity lens, which states, "Through strengthening our SEL competencies we are better able to connect across race, class, gender identity, sexual orientation, learning needs, and age."

Educational equity means that every student receives what they need in order to develop their full academic, social, and emotional potential despite race, gender, ethnicity, language, disability, family background, or family income. In addition to allocating resources equitably, we must also have an understanding of critical race theory and interrupt practices that are inequitable so we can create more inclusive school environments. As a person of color, I know firsthand how important it is for educators to recognize the legacy of racism in our schools if we are to really support our students' SEL. In an August 2018 *Education Week* commentary, LaShawn Routé Chatmon and Kathleen Osta remind us that our context in the United States has always been racialized, and our race impacts our access to opportunities and how we experience the world:

> From the beginning, schools in the United States were designed to benefit and affirm the values and culture of the white people in power. Over time, this white dominant culture shaped the educational structures and policies that articulate how children are expected to behave, communicate, and interact. Today, how learning is organized and evaluated is still rooted in an acceptance of whiteness as "natural" and "normal." The presumption that students from a culture outside this "norm" come to school with deficits—in

their intelligence, families, culture, or communities—is built into the DNA of public education. (Chatmon & Osta, 2018)

The city of Oakland, which I serve, ranges from affluent hill communities to the flatlands by the waters of the San Francisco Bay. Over the years as our SEL team began holding a racial equity lens more closely to our work, we saw that in schools with a majority of students of color SEL was often being identified solely as a self-management skill to address classroom behavior problems, while in our hill schools SEL was being viewed as delivering twenty-first-century skills for success. As a result, our team made a presentation at a CASEL Collaborating District's gathering around how SEL and mindfulness are often taken up as behavior management tools in schools with predominantly black and brown children. This professional learning helped spark a growing conversation within CASEL around SEL and equity.

CASEL convened an Equity Working Group to examine how transformative SEL can be an avenue for creating greater educational equity. Transformative SEL encourages us to be mindful of when SEL is reduced solely to an "intervention to address the perceived deficits of students of color or students living in poverty while ignoring the impact of inequities in our systems" and really utilize SEL as a force for developing "student agency to lead positive change in their own communities" (Chatmon & Osta, 2018). Transformative SEL is informed by interconnectedness and awareness of structural inequities while also including practices that are culturally responsive, incorporate student voice, and promote social justice. Currently, CASEL is refining equity elaborations to their framework and exploring how SEL can truly be culturally responsive and deepen our understanding of racial stress, systemic oppression, and implicit bias.

Equity-Elaborated CASEL Competencies

In November of 2018, Vice President of Research for CASEL, Robert Jagers, along with Deborah Rivas-Drake and Teresa Borowski, published a brief—*Equity & Social and Emotional Learning: A Cultural Analysis*—that analyzes the potential concerns and opportunities when one holds an equity lens to the five CASEL competencies. In this important brief, the authors also share proposed revisions to recent definitions of CASEL core competencies to include equity elaborations. While this work around SEL and equity is dynamic and very much in development, in December of 2018, I had the privilege to present on behalf of CASEL with Rob Jagers and CASEL Consultant, Mary Hurley, on *Social Emotional Learning in Service of Equitable Outcomes* at Learning Forward in Dallas, Texas where we had participants engage with the equity elaborations shared below. You will also see how Oakland's SEL standards (also shared below) aim to embed an equity lens.

• SELF-AWARENESS

Involves understanding one's emotions, personal identity, goals, and values. This includes accurately assessing one's strengths and limitations, having positive mindsets, possessing a well-grounded sense of self-efficacy and optimism. High levels of self-awareness require the ability to understand the links between one's personal and sociocultural identities and to recognize how thoughts, feelings, and actions are interconnected.

• SELF-MANAGEMENT

Requires skills and attitudes that facilitate the ability to regulate emotions and behaviors. This includes the ability to delay gratification, manage stress, control impulses, and persevere through personal and group-level challenges in order to achieve personal and educational goals.

• SOCIAL AWARENESS

Involves the ability to take the perspective of those with the same and different backgrounds and cultures and to empathize and feel compassion. It also involves understanding social norms for behavior in diverse settings and recognizing family, school, and community resources and supports.

• RELATIONSHIP SKILLS

Includes the tools needed to establish and maintain healthy and rewarding relationships, and to e ectively navigate settings with di ering social norms and demands. It involves communicating clearly, listening actively, cooperating, resisting inappropriate social pressure, negotiating conflict constructively, and seeking help when it is needed.

• RESPONSIBLE DECISION-MAKING

Requires the knowledge, skills, and attitudes to make caring, constructive choices about personal behavior and social interactions across diverse settings. It requires the ability to critically examine ethical standards, safety concerns, and behavioral norms for risky behavior; to make realistic evaluations of consequences of various interpersonal and institutional actions; and to take the health and well-being of self and others into consideration.

GOING DEEPER

Valuable resources to deepen the conversation around SEL and equity:

1. "Pursuing Social and Emotional Development Through a Racial Equity Lens: A Call to Action" (Aspen Institute, 2018)

2. "Pursuing Social and Emotional Development Through a Racial Equity Lens: 5 Strategies for System Leaders to Take Action" (Aspen Institute, 2018)

3. Social-Emotional Learning & Equity Pitfalls and Recommendations (National Equity Project in collaboration with the Aspen Institute, 2018)

4. Equity & Social and Emotional Learning: A Cultural Analysis (Borowski, Jagers, Rivas-Drake, 2018)

5. Mindful of Race: Transforming Racism from the Inside Out (King, 2018)

SEL and Cultural Responsiveness

SEL and culturally responsive teaching both seek to address educational inequity. The Center for Reaching and Teaching the Whole Child is engaged in powerful work supporting teacher education while bringing together these two

ANCHOR STANDARD		LEARNING STANDARD
1. Self-Awareness Develop and demonstrate self awareness skills to: • Identify personal, cultural, and linguistic assets • Identify prejudices and biases towards people different than oneself • Understand the connections between one's emotions, social contexts and identity • Demonstrate an accurate self-concept based on one's strengths and challenges • Identify when help is needed and who can provide it	1A	Individual demonstrates an understanding of one's emotions.
	1B	Individual demonstrates knowledge of personal strengths, challenges, cultural, linguistic assets, and aspirations.
	1C	Individual demonstrates awareness of personal rights and responsibilities.
	1D	Individual demonstrates an awareness of when help is needed and who can provide it.
2.Self- Management Develop and demonstrate self-management skills to: • Regulate one's emotions and behaviors in contexts with people different than oneself • Motivate oneself to set and achieve goals	2A	Individual demonstrates the skills to manage and express one's emotions, thoughts, impulses and stress in constructive ways.
	2B	Individual demonstrates the skills to set, monitor, adapt, achieve, and evaluate goals.
3. Social Awareness Develop and demonstrate social awareness skills to: • Establish and maintain healthy interactions and relationships across diverse communities • Embrace diversity and take the perspectives of people different from oneself • Demonstrate empathy for people similar to and different from oneself	3A	Individual demonstrates empathy for other people's emotions, perspectives, cultures, languages, and histories.
	3B	Individual contributes productively to one's school, workplace, and community.
	3C	Individual demonstrates an awareness
	3D	Individual recognizes leadership capacity in themselves and others.

ANCHOR STANDARD		LEARNING STANDARD
4. Relationship Skills Develop and demonstrate relationship skills to: • Relate to people similar to and different than oneself • Communicate clearly and effectively • Build, establish and maintain healthy relationship	4A	Individual uses a range of communication skills to interact effectively with individuals of diverse backgrounds, abilities, languages, and lifestyles
	4B	Individual cultivates constructive relationships with individuals of diverse backgrounds, abilities, languages, and lifestyles.
	4C	Individual demonstrates skills to respectfully engage in and resolve interpersonal conflicts in various contexts.
5. Responsible Decision Making Develop and demonstrate responsible decision-making skills to: • Problem solve effectively while being respectful of people similar to and different from oneself • Behave responsibly in personal, professional, and community contexts • Make constructive and respectful choices that consider the well-being of self and others.	5A	Individual considers the well-being of self and others when making decisions.
	5B	Individual uses a systematic approach to decision making in a variety of situations.
	5C	Individual applies problem-solving skills to engage responsibly in a variety of situations.

FIGURE 1.2: Oakland Unified School District PreK–Adult Social and Emotional Learning Standards

Oakland Unified School District Office of Social and Emotional Learning fields. They have developed anchor competencies and corresponding teacher moves that integrate culturally responsive teaching into what they call the social-emotional dimension of teaching and learning (learn more at http://crtwc.org/).

GOING DEEPER

An important resource on culturally responsive teaching is *Culturally Responsive Teaching and the Brain: Promoting Authentic Engagement and Rigor Among Culturally and Linguistically Diverse Students* by Zaretta Hammond.

Hammond writes "culturally responsive teaching emphasizes cultural ways of learning and cognition rather than focusing on cosmetic "race related" displays. Affirmation of students' cultural roots comes through incorporating deep cultural values and cultural ways of learning (using the memory systems of the brain, organizing around social interaction (collectivism), and combining oratory skills with academic talk) rather than through superficial pictures of "heroes" or images of Africa or Mexico or irrelevant mentioning in the curriculum" (2015).

SEL and Mindful Awareness Practices

Mindful awareness practices (MAPs) are exercises that promote a state of heightened and receptive attention to moment-by-moment experience (Bishop et al., 2004; Siegel, 2007). Several practices or exercises are thought to increase this state of awareness including forms of meditation, yoga, and Tai-Chi (Allen, Blashki, and Gullone, 2006; Wall, 2005). A common exercise involves directing the attention to a present experience or sensation such as the movement of the belly during in-and-out breaths. Quite often the attention will wander periodically from its target object and a conscious recognition of this lapse in attention allows for the refocusing of awareness and drawing attention back to the chosen experience. Practicing mindfulness is likened to practicing a sport or playing a musical instrument, in that proficiency is cultivated through repetition and continuous practice. (Flook et al., 2010)

In my work in Oakland, I've seen how several mindful awareness practice (MAP) program providers often use MAPs and SEL interchangeably, but MAPs are in fact not a comprehensive approach to SEL. Rather, mindful awareness practices can be a powerful complementary approach to enhance and reinforce comprehensive social and emotional learning as long as MAPs do not focus exclusively on self-regulation and instead lead to greater social awareness. Throughout this book and in my work, I incorporate MAPs and offer some helpful insights into teaching in these overlapping but distinct areas. A great way to understand the relationship between SEL and MAPs is a sports analogy first suggested by Dinabandhu Sarley of the 1440 Foundation at a 2015 CASEL meeting that brought together several experts and program providers in the fields of SEL and MAPs to explore the relationships between the two. In sports, effective training usually involves two key elements: (1) learning and practice, and (2) physical conditioning. SEL consists of learning and practice, and MAPs promote mental fitness, which enhances learning. MAPs have the capacity to assist students in calming themselves and focusing their attention, thus creating conditions for academic learning, as well as social and emotional learning. Additionally, the calmer, more focused mental state potentially achieved through MAPs may help students be less anxious and reactive so they can develop positive, healthy relationships with teachers and peers (Dusenbury, Sarley, Weissberg, & Domitrovich, 2016), which in turn enhances SEL.

MAPs are also increasingly part of teacher wellness initiatives in schools and school districts, and there is growing research on how growing MAPs in teachers can positively influence their teaching practice and lead to increased teacher happiness and retention.

Other SEL Frameworks

If you feel the CASEL framework doesn't fit your context, I encourage you to explore the following frameworks:

- The University of Chicago Consortium on School Research's Foundations for Young Adult Success (https://consortium.uchicago.edu/publications/foundations-young-adult-success-developmental-framework)
- Turnaround for Children's Building Blocks for Learning (https://www.turnaroundusa.org/what-we-do/tools/building-blocks/)

- Partnership for 21st Century Learning (P21) Framework (http://www.p21.org/our-work/p21-framework)
- Engaging Schools, Learning and Life Competencies (https://engagingschools.org/)
- Valor Collegiate Academy's Compass (https://valorcollegiate.org/compass/compass/)

GOING DEEPER

Stephanie Jones and her team at the Harvard Graduate School of Education identify three main areas of SEL skills:

- **Cognitive regulation skills.** Also called executive function skills, this bucket includes working memory, cognitive flexibility, inhibitory control, and attention control.
- **Emotion skills.** This group includes emotion knowledge and expression, emotion behavior and regulation, and empathy and perspective taking.
- **Interpersonal skills.** Also called the social domain, this bucket includes prosocial behaviors and skills, the ability to understand social cues, and conflict resolution.

(Shafer, 2016)

The Social, Emotional, and Ethical Learning Framework

The social, emotional, and ethical (SEE) learning conceptual framework is currently being developed by the Center for Contemplative Science and Compassion-Based Ethics at Emory University. It integrates components that have been suggested by some of the founders of CASEL but are not often found explicitly in SEL. These components include attention, ethics grounded in compassion and kindness, and a systems approach that explores how we exist within and are affected by interdependent systems. This framework can be useful in promoting MAPs and a reconnection with ecological values where humans have a more sacred relationship with the earth engaging in inquiry around the root cause of unsustainable practices while exploring conservation and the restoration of ecosystems (see http://www.dalailama.emory.edu/center/).

Dispelling the False Dichotomy Between SEL and Academics

It is neurobiologically impossible to build memories, engage complex thoughts, or make meaningful decisions without emotion.

—Mary Helen Immordino-Yang

One of my pet peeves is when someone refers to SEL as "soft skills" or noncognitive skills—learning is social and emotional! In fact, education thought leader and college readiness expert David T. Conley (2013) advocated for replacing the term "noncognitive" with "metacognitive": the mind's ability to reflect on how effectively it is handling the learning process as it is doing so. American education scholar Mike Rose (2013) proposed utilizing the full meaning of cognition—"one that is robust and intellectual, intimately connected to character and social development, and directed toward the creation of a better world."

We now know that academic skills are intertwined with SEL skills. In "The Evidence Base for How We Learn," distinguished scientists from several fields developed a consensus statement "affirming the interconnectedness of social, emotional, and cognitive development as central to the learning process" (Jones & Kahn, 2017). Research confirms that when classrooms connect rigorous cognitive challenges with social interaction or ignite emotions, it results in deeper learning (Jones & Kahn, 2017). Just as effective student learning is connected to SEL, successful teaching must also weave SEL into instruction. Think back to your favorite classes when you were an adolescent. What factors made the class your favorite? Chances are, your teacher was able to connect emotionally with your class; there may have been a certain degree of risk taking and engagement, and in order to take risks and stay engaged you had to feel safe, seen, and connected—all of which are attributes of SEL.

In *The Practice Base for How We Learn*, distinguished educators from across the United States developed consensus statements around the practice of integrating SEL. These educators affirm that how we teach is just as important as what we teach and call for both explicit and embedded SEL instruction along with caring classrooms and schools in order to develop SEL. "Just as the culture of the classroom must reflect social belonging and emotional safety, so can academic instruction embody and enhance these competencies and be enhanced by them" (Berman, Chaffee, & Sarmiento, 2018). Integrating SEL shifts the emphasis to the learning environment, whereas before curricular content was the main focus. It also presents an opportunity to focus more on equity, where "learning opportunities are inclusive of and responsive to the diversity of interests, aptitudes, perspectives, races, and cultures represented in the classroom" (Berman et al., 2018). To promote deeper learning, SEL can't be approached as an add-on or discrete intervention. It must be an integral part of the academic program with the foundational understanding that SEL and academics reinforce each other.

> *[SEL] is not a detour from a pursuit of academics, it's an on-ramp.*
> —Jeff Wagenheim

One of my most rewarding experiences in Oakland was providing SEL-targeted professional learning for all of the vice principals in our district. As a result of our professional learning, one of these leaders wanted SEL to be prioritized more highly at his school. During one of our meetings, he expressed frustration with his principal and instructional leadership team, and shared how the focus was solely on academic rigor. I listened to this leader intently and, after he shared that the overemphasis on academics was at the cost of compassion, I asked him to reflect on the skills students needed in order to succeed at the academic tasks his principal and leadership team focused on. In his sharing, he realized that several of the skills were actually SEL skills (e.g., reflection, perseverance, focus). We spent the rest of the meeting strategizing how he could help his colleagues see how interdependent SEL is with academic learning and how essential SEL is to create optimal conditions for learning. This leader left our meeting understanding that there isn't a choice to make between compassion or rigor but that it can (in fact it has to) be both.

With the advent of the Common Core State Standards (which have been adopted by forty-six states and the District of Columbia), critical thinking and problem solving have become central to learning and success. These skills require healthy social and emotional development—SEL skills support how students learn. These standards either explicitly mention SEL skills, or SEL skills are implicit in the standards, and a deep understanding of SEL is critical in seeing the connection. For example, the speaking and listening standards call for effective participation in a "range of conversations and collaborations with diverse partners, building on others' ideas and expressing their own clearly and persuasively" (Common Core State Standards Initiative, n.d.). While the SEL skills of self-awareness, relationship skills, and social awareness are critical to meeting this standard, this connection may not be obvious to an educator who has not yet received SEL-targeted professional development.

Why Is SEL Critical for Adolescents?

Defined as the period between puberty and adulthood, adolescence is a time of intense physical, emotional, and social changes. Often more time is spent with friends than family, and there are higher levels of potentially risky behavior. The 2013 Centers for Disease Control Youth Risk Behavior Surveillance System reported that 35% of survey participants had consumed alcohol, 23% had used marijuana, 16% had smoked cigarettes, 47% had been sexually active, 8% had attempted suicide in the past year, and morbidity and mortality rates increased by 200% (CDC, 2014). These data alone should be enough to convince middle and high schools to prioritize SEL so that their students develop the skills and competencies to ultimately make healthier choices. Research also shows that the transition to middle school often comes with decreased motivation, confidence, attention, and self-esteem along with organizational challenges—these are all issues that SEL addresses directly.

The Adolescent Brain and SEL

When I was in the classroom, I often showed my students *Frontline*'s *Inside the Teenage Brain* (Spinks, 2002) to help them understand from a neurological perspective why SEL is important to develop, especially during adolescence. The part of our brain responsible for effective planning, reasoning, and self-regulating, the prefrontal cortex, is the last to mature, and research shows that while adults use this part of their brain for most of their decision making, teens tend to use the back of their brain or the limbic system (Spinks, 2002). In fact, during adolescence the limbic system is developing more quickly than the prefrontal cortex, and it seeks stimulus through things like social media, parties, athletics, gossip, and sexual experiences, which can provide quick and easy stimulation, but not all of these activities are safe, and adolescents don't always reflect on safety when they are seeking excitement (Elias, 2018). Instead of waiting until the frontal lobe is more developed, adolescence is actually an optimal time to teach SEL so young people can make healthier choices. In fact, emotional intelligence expert Maurice Elias (2018) argues that "since the brain is most malleable while it is growing and developing we have not only an opportunity but an obligation to promote self-understanding, self-control, and good choices."

While the teen brain matures it's also more vulnerable to stress, which can overload the frontal lobe. Studies show that when teens learn how to de-stress and engage in self-reflection, they can improve the function of their frontal lobe and show not only improved self-regulation but also improved cognition and working memory, which contributes to academic performance (Davidson, 2008).

Success and Readiness for College and Career

While the national high school graduation and college enrollment rates are on the rise, a discouragingly low percentage of these students receive a bachelor's degree within 6 years—59% (National Center for Education Statistics, n.d.).

SEL is critical to college and career preparation and success. In *Improving College and Career Readiness by Incorporating Social and Emotional Learning*, the authors detail how each competency in the CASEL framework relates to college and career readiness (Dymnicki, Sambolt, & Kidron, 2013). Some examples below:

Self-awareness: Connects to an individual's perception of his or her own ability to accomplish a goal or execute a plan and has been shown to shape long-term aspirations and career trajectories.

Self-management: Supports stress management and enables students to handle emotions such as test anxiety as they engage in more challenging coursework in high school and college. Students who can manage stress more effectively have been found to transition to college with more success and stronger academic records (DeBerard, Spielmans, & Julka, 2004).

Social awareness: Builds ability to identify situations in which social support can serve as a resource for managing problems. For example, parental and peer support during the transition to college is key in reducing anxiety and meeting new academic demands.

Relationship skills: Enables students to work with others from different cultures and backgrounds, helps them build new social networks in college, and know how to seek out counselors, faculty members, and other support services. Being connected to supportive peers can reduce feelings of loneliness and increase college retention.

Responsible decision-making: Improves systematic reasoning ability and provides adolescents with the ability to imagine future outcomes, allowing them to determine the consequences of their actions.

Improving College and Career Readiness by Incorporating Social and Emotional Learning (Dymnicki et al., 2013)

SEL for Adolescents

In the *Future of Children*, David Yeager (2017) found that while SEL programs that directly teach skills may be effective with children, they are not as effective with middle adolescents (roughly ages 14–17). Yeager's findings suggest that strong SEL programming for adolescents must focus on mind-sets and climates where students feel respected by their teachers and classmates. Yeager cautions against revamping elementary skills-based SEL programs for teens and instead advises that effective SEL approaches with adolescents must occur in respectful environments where young people can connect to what they value. He discusses one study that gave students in an academically demanding class more choice in what they would work on; after enjoying a stronger sense of agency, students were less likely to be disciplined. Consistent with Yeager's findings, positive teacher-student relationships (Pianta et al., 2012) and classrooms where students feel seen, heard, connected with peers, and involved in decision making result in more motivation and stronger academic performance (NSCC, 2007).

> If we define successful SEL programs as those that instruct and expect adolescents to apply a given skill in novel settings and thereby show greater well-being, then the evidence is discouraging, but if we include programs that affect social-emotional outcomes by creating climates and mindsets that help adolescents cope more successfully with the challenges they encounter, then evidence is not only encouraging but demands urgent action in schools across the country. (Yeager, 2017)

Yeager's analysis is welcome in the structure of middle and high school, which doesn't always allow for implementation of a stand-alone skills-based SEL program. Moreover, in CASEL's 2015 review of effective SEL programs for secondary schools, four out of the five recommended high school SEL programs did not have stand-alone SEL lessons but rather focused on teaching practices that centered on cultivating positive relationships, student voice and choice, and personalized student supports. This book offers guidance on how to create a classroom that incorporates these practices.

Students Want SEL

In November of 2018, a report for CASEL, *Respected: Perspectives of Youth on High School & Social and Emotional Learning*, found that students feel unprepared for life after high school due to a lack of social and emotional skills development (Atwell, Bridgeland, DePaoli, Shriver). This report along with findings from The Aspen Institute Youth Commission on Social, Emotional, and Academic Development calls upon adults and schools to treat adolescents as whole learners.

SEL Every Day seeks to lift up this Youth Call to Action (2018) by providing educators with the tools to start prioritizing SEL in service of:

1. Providing safety and building community in classrooms and schools.
2. Knowing and understanding students.
3. Creating environments where students can learn and be evaluated as whole students and whole people.
4. Embracing families and communities as partners in learning.

GOING DEEPER

1. *Respected: Perspectives of Youth on High School & Social and Emotional Learning* (Atwell, Bridgeland, DePaoli, Shriver, 2018)
2. *In Support of How We Learn: A Youth Call to Action* (Aspen Institute, 2018).

How to Use This Book

If the kids don't know you're doing it [SEL], you're not doing it.
> —Linda Carlson, Anchorage School District, assistant superintendent

Now that you know what SEL is and why it is especially important for secondary students, it's time to dive into exactly how you can start to incorporate SEL into your teaching practice. You are likely already incorporating a lot of SEL but haven't necessarily been naming it, and a key focus of this book is the importance of naming what you are doing and being intentional with SEL in both the planning and execution of your teaching.

Each of the following chapters starts with an educator story about SEL within the context of the chapter focus. Chapters may also include:

- *Note from the Field*, which highlights on-the-ground SEL work.
- *Going Deeper*, which lifts up relevant research and resources for further exploration.
- *Practices*, which help cultivate SEL in teachers and teaching practices that promote SEL in students (see chapters 2 and 3).
- *Starting Where You Are*, which offers suggestions on where to start incorporating what's been presented in each chapter.

Chapter 2 discusses the importance of building community in the secondary context and offers SEL practices to help sustain a respectful, warm, and engaging classroom and create conditions for learning. Chapter 3 focuses specifically on teaching practices that promote SEL, such as academic discussion, cooperative learning, student voice and self-assessment, and also shows how SEL is integral to the Common Core. Chapter 4 provides instruction on how to make SEL explicit in lesson planning and provides examples of incorporating SEL in learning targets and content. Chapter 5 focuses on reflective practice, the ability to reflect on one's actions so as to engage in a process of continuous learning, and offers resources for teachers to employ an inquiry-based approach to their instruction and use data to see how they are making an impact. In the afterword, I invite readers to think about love as the ultimate goal of SEL and our work as educators. Finally, there is an appendix that details recommended resources.

A note here about what this book is and what it isn't. This book offers guidance on how to be more intentional about SEL in academic instruction and how to incorporate SEL teaching practices. This book is not a skills-based SEL curriculum that offers lessons to directly teach specific skills, and it should not be used in place of an evidence-based SEL program. If your school is also implementing an evidence-based SEL program, it is advised that you reinforce the specific SEL skills and competencies taught in that program through your academic content and instruction in a systematic way. Also, this book is not an exhaustive resource on integrating SEL with academic instruction. Rather, it is a practical guide and accessible starting point for educators on how to begin teaching with SEL in mind in middle and high school settings.

Creating Community: The Relationship-Centered Classroom

I've come to a frightening conclusion that I am the decisive element in the classroom. It's my personal approach that creates the climate. It's my daily mood that makes the weather. As a teacher, I possess a tremendous power to make a child's life miserable or joyous. I can be a tool of torture or an instrument of inspiration. I can humiliate or heal. In all situations, it is my response that decides whether a crisis will be escalated or de-escalated and a child humanized or dehumanized.

—Haim Ginott

During my time serving as a district administrator in Oakland schools, I've had the opportunity to work with many teachers who prioritize relationships. Californians for Justice (CFJ)—an inspiring, statewide grassroots organization working for racial justice by building the power of youth, immigrants, low-income families, communities of color, and LGBTQ communities—engaged more than 2,000 students and 65 education leaders on what students needed to be prepared for college, careers, and community life. They found a perhaps surprising common factor for success: more than access to technology, for example, it was the relationships between students and staff that were the key to success in and after high school. This is consistent with research findings that effective SEL approaches in middle and high schools help adolescents to feel respected by both adults and peers (Yeager, 2017); students who respect and value themselves and others are more likely to create functional learning environments.

HIGH SCHOOL ENGLISH LANGUAGE LEARNER TEACHER

I teach in a school for new immigrants to the United States. My students are from over 40 countries and speak more than 30 languages. All of my students qualify for free and reduced lunch, and they are dealing with the trauma that comes with immigration.

For me, teaching is all about relationships, being present, helping my students make connections, and creating a safe space so students are able to learn whatever the content is. Instead of prioritizing how quickly I could get a lesson started, I began prioritizing how I could get my students ready to learn, and this has made all the difference. Before students come into the room, I greet each one individually (this is also my opportunity to have them locate their cell phone and put it away in their bag so it won't be a distraction during class) and make eye contact. I can see in their eyes if something is wrong and make a note to check in with them. Every class starts with practicing mindfulness, and this gives us a chance to ground ourselves and transition to being fully present in class, which is especially important amid the hectic pace that comes with living in New York City. This time is crucial for me too; there are so many things that can pull my attention away (papers in need of grading stacked on my desk, emails to return, and lessons to plan), and taking this time enables me to better connect with my students.

Giving up the first 10 minutes of my class to intentionally create conditions for learning through individually greeting each student and de-stressing and centering with mindfulness, I make up that time a million-fold because we are less likely to have to stop because of off-task behavior. Once we ground ourselves, I ensure that instruction integrates SEL and builds community and connection in the classroom. I have my students engage in a learning activity I call people to people, where I offer a prompt related to the content we are studying and invite my students to find a partner who doesn't speak their native language to discuss the prompt. This will get my students moving around the classroom to find new partners and has them practice active listening, because I have each one paraphrase what their partner said.

Julie Mann, Newcomers High School, Long Island City, NY

Efforts by CFJ included observing the interactions of 51 Oakland high school students with teachers and staff over the course of a single day. While some of their findings were promising, the reality is that one out of three students in California cannot identify a single caring adult at school (California Healthy Kids Survey, 2015). As a result, CFJ launched a campaign to promote relationship-centered schools that focus primarily on integrating SEL into school life.

Research suggests that teachers' SEL skills are an important predictor of the quality of teacher-student relationships and the culture and climate in a classroom (Jones, Bouffard, & Weissbourd, 2013, 63). This chapter highlights some key ways teachers can build their own SEL muscle along with some important teaching practices that aid in creating and sustaining community and the conditions for a relationship-centered classroom. While this chapter focuses primarily on cultivating relationships with young people in a classroom context, I encourage you to reflect on how you can develop positive relationships with parents and community members as well so you can all partner together in service of SEL.

Creating Community Starts With You: The Role of Mindfulness

No significant learning occurs without a significant relationship.
—Dr. James Comer

There are a few brilliant souls to whom I often turn for guidance. Some of these individuals are present-day mentors I can call on the phone or meet for coffee, and others are inspiring thought leaders I try to summon and connect with through their writing. One of these is the great, late Dr. Maya Angelou, who overcame grinding poverty and abuse in her youth to become one of the United States' most celebrated writers. Her heartful wisdom and understanding of human relationships never cease to amaze and move me. I recently came across an article that shared four critical questions Dr. Angelou felt we unconsciously ask each other all the time (Schafler, 2017):

1. Do you see me?
2. Do you care that I'm here?
3. Am I enough for you, or do you need me to be better in some way?
4. Can I tell that I'm special to you by the way that you look at me?

These questions speak to me from a personal perspective as a new parent and a partner; they underline how critical our relationships are for cultivating a deep sense of connection. As an educator, I also immediately see how foundational these questions are to create a sense of safety and connection in the classroom; the degree to which our students feel truly seen influences their well-being and also their academic engagement. Just think of Julie's story from the start of the chapter.

In order to answer these four questions for our students, we have to be fully present and available for them. As teachers, the greatest gift we can offer our students is our presence and our ability to really see them. Haim

Ginott wisely reminds us that we are the "decisive element" when teaching, and our own states of mind ripple throughout our classrooms. But how can we best provide our students (and indeed all the people in our lives) with the gifts of our presence and vision?

One of the most powerful ways to be present and cultivate what Roeser, Skinner, Beers, and Jennings (2012) refer to as "habits of mind" or dispositions, such as awareness, attention, flexibility, and intentionality, is to develop a personal mindfulness practice (Jones, Bouffard, & Weissbourd, 2013, 63). Mindfulness has garnered a lot of attention in recent years, particularly in the fields of mental health and education. After all, teaching is a high-stress profession.

Between 1985 and 2012, the percentage of teachers who experienced high stress during a majority of their week increased from 35% to 51% (Eva & Thayer, 2017). Teacher wellness has increasingly become a focus for schools seeking to boost their faculty retention rates. Nationally schools lose between $1 billion and $2.2 billion in attrition costs each year through teachers moving or leaving the profession (Alliance for Excellent Education, 2014).

Emerging empirical research that has been conducted on applications of mindfulness training for educators using a randomized, controlled design points to improvements across a range of measures including reduced stress and burnout, increased mindfulness, improved attention, and more effective organization of classroom time (Flook, Goldberg, Pinger, Bonus, & Davidson, 2013; Jennings et al., 2017; Kemeny et al., 2012; Roeser et al., 2013). In

"The Mindful Teacher: Translating Research Into Daily Well-Being," Eva and Thayer (2017) discuss the research base for mindfulness, highlight educator resources to support stress management, and emphasize the importance of having a consistent and frequent practice.

There are a number of excellent resources geared toward teachers to help support the development of a personal mindfulness practice (see recommended resources in the appendix). What follows are wellness practices you can explore immediately, including mindful breathing, doing one activity daily with mindfulness, seeing oneself in others (particularly your students), and understanding your emotions. All of the following practices also strengthen our adult SEL competencies. For example, mindful breathing can deepen our self-awareness and self-management skills, and seeing oneself in others can generate empathy and improve our relationship skills. There is increasing interest in developing mindfulness and SEL simultaneously and in how each approach can reinforce and enhance the other.

GOING DEEPER

Lantieri and Zakrzewski (2015) help distinguish between SEL and mindfulness: "To start, SEL uses an outside-in approach with a focus on teaching skills: a teacher introduces a skill such as recognizing an emotion or using 'I' messages, the students practice it for a set amount of time, and then the teacher moves on to the next skill. SEL assumes that this process is enough to enable students to use the skill in all relevant, real-life situations. Mindfulness, on the other hand, works from the inside out, drawing on the premise that each person has the innate capacity for relationship-building qualities such as empathy and kindness—a premise that research now supports."

Practice: Mindful Breathing

Your breath is always with you. Observing the breath is one of the easiest, simplest ways to start practicing mindfulness and establish your mind and body in the present moment. Many times we may be physically present but our minds are elsewhere, and bringing conscious awareness to our breathing can help us unite our minds with our bodies. Mindful breathing can be done anytime, anywhere. By bringing awareness to your breathing, you can gently bring a wandering mind back to the present moment. Practicing mindful breathing is a wonderful way to de-stress and replenish ourselves. Whenever you are in line somewhere, for example, while waiting to use the bathroom, at the supermarket, or in your car at a stoplight, you can use this time to come back to yourself and practice mindful breathing.

There are a number of helpful apps that can help you get started. One that I often recommend is the Insight Timer app, which has a number of guided mindful breathing exercises and a timer with various bells or chimes that you can set for the amount of time you wish to practice.

Here are some quick directions to help you get started:

- Find a comfortable seated position where your back is straight but at ease. Sit either on a comfortable cushion on the floor with your knees below your diaphragm or in a chair with your feet grounded to the floor.
- Place your hand on your abdomen or chest so you can feel your body expand and contract with your breaths.
- Your mind will wander; this is the nature of the mind. Just try your best to focus on the sensation of your breaths and fully feel each inhale and exhale.
- Sometimes it's helpful to coordinate your breath with a silent affirmation, a positive statement or word. For example, on the in-breath silently say "calm"; on the out-breath silently say "peace." Use whatever word or phrase nourishes you.
- Start with just 5 minutes a day and gradually increase your practice by 5 minutes each week.

Practice: One Daily Activity Done
With Mindfulness and the Three Ts

Whether it's tying your shoes, walking the path from the parking lot to your classroom, or one of your daily meals, choosing one activity to engage in mindfully can be very nourishing to your ability to pay attention and see things with fresh eyes.

The Three Ts refers to tea time, transitional time, and toilet time. Teachers can choose one of the Ts to engage in mindfully.

- Through simply engaging in mindful breathing and truly tasting our tea or coffee, we can practice mindfulness in the staff room during our breaks.
- Transitional time refers to all the time we spend waiting, in line at the grocery store, in traffic, and so on.
- If we live to be 70 years old, we will have spent three years of our lives waiting! Imagine if that time had been spent practicing mindfulness. Depending on how long our trips to the bathroom last, we could spend between one and a half and four years on the toilet—and often for teachers this is the only time we get to be alone during the school day. Everyone has to use the bathroom. Relieving ourselves instantly brings us back into our bodies, presenting a ripe opportunity to practice mindfulness.

As a busy teacher I used the bell that signals the end of class as a mindfulness bell and a reminder to come back to my breath. I also incorporated mindful breathing into wait time when I offered my students thinking time to reflect on and then answer a prompt.

Practice: Seeing Oneself in Others

Seeing students, colleagues, and parents as you see yourself increases compassion, altruism, and prosocial behavior—essential qualities for a thriving school community. In preparation for classes, faculty meetings, and parent conferences, try to see yourself as your students, your colleagues, or the parents of your students. Try to put yourself in their shoes. This practice can help you gain perspective and go into your class, meeting, or conference with much more ease. For example, if a student acts up, first try to remember what it was like for you when you were an adolescent, and then put yourself in your student's shoes as much as you can.

Here are some sentence stems to help you think about how you can really bring this into your teaching practice:

- "Breathing in, I see myself as the parent of _____ [student's name]. Breathing out, I recognize we are a team and we want the best for _____ [student's name]."
- "Breathing in, I see myself as _____ [student name]. Breathing out, I recognize that _____ [student name] wants to be seen, heard, and valued."

- "Breathing in, I see myself as _____ [colleague's name]. Breathing out, I recognize that _____ [colleague's name] wants what's best for their students.

Practice: You Are Not Your Emotion

Throughout the course of the day, we experience a wide variety of emotions. Engaging in mindfulness as we practice mindful breathing, we bring a kind, curious attention to what we are experiencing in the moment. So when an emotion arises, we find out what it is. What am I feeling now? Anger? Sadness? Frustration? Once we name the emotion, we are able to tame it and create space between ourselves and the emotion we are experiencing. We can engage in an inquiry about the emotion even further by checking in to see where in our body we are feeling the emotion. For example, "I'm feeling tight in my chest as I go into this staff meeting." We can go further into this inquiry by reflecting on why the emotion is visiting us and ask it what it needs. Through engaging with the emotion in this way, the intensity of the emotion lessens and we are better able to manage strong emotions. Mindfulness helps us cultivate a curious attitude to our internal and external experiences, and through holding a stance of curiosity we can ask questions that help us broaden our perspective and be less reactive.

Sharing Mindfulness With Young People

While there is a growing amount of research to support bringing mindfulness into the classroom, important research questions remain unanswered, including (1) the developmental appropriateness of strategies at different ages, (2) the intensity and duration necessary to improve student functioning, and (3) whether there is a lasting effect at least one or two years following these interventions (CASEL, 2015).

Mindfulness has the capacity to help students manage stress, regulate their emotions, and focus their attention so they can be available for academic, social, and emotional learning. Several evidence-based SEL programs have already begun incorporating mindfulness into their programming. While many of these programs lack a daily mindfulness practice component, the fact that well-established evidence-based SEL programs are incorporating mindfulness signals the growing importance of these practices to the SEL field.

While there's been tremendous growth in the number of educators who are trained in mindfulness and consequently also in the number of students who receive mindfulness instruction, there are also significant concerns around mindfulness being used solely as a behavior management tool. Mindfulness is often marketed as something that will help get your students to self-regulate and behave. While it is true that mindfulness practices can support students in developing self-regulation, these practices are so much more than that. They can help grow compassion and altruism, and ultimately give practitioners insight into themselves at a deep level. Once you have developed your own practice, you can start to explore sharing mindfulness with your students in ways that feel authentic to you.

GOING DEEPER

In *Education as the Practice of Freedom: A Social Justice Proposal for Mindfulness Educators*, Jennifer Cannon (2016) discusses how when "mindfulness is divorced from a social justice foundation it can be manipulated as a tool of the neoliberal market to improve test scores, increase attention, or control student behavior. At best, mindfulness education can help provide our students with a foundation of inner peace, calm and centered awareness, and offer a reprieve from self-defeating thoughts. If we integrate principles of compassion, interconnection, and solidarity along with concrete pathways to enact these principles in service to community empowerment and social justice, then we are birthing a new paradigm in mindfulness education" and one that aligns with transformative SEL.

Building Community: Restorative Practices and the Power of Circles

Restorative Practices (RP), often used interchangeably with Restorative Justice (RJ), are specific practices inspired by indigenous values that build community, respond to harm or conflict, and provide circles of support for community members. These practices seek to support collectivist values in the classroom while utilizing a structure that emphasizes interdependence. By building, maintaining, and restoring relationships between members of the entire school community, RJ helps to create an environment where all students can thrive.

Since 2011, RJ has helped to decrease suspensions in the Oakland Unified School District by half. Students who consistently experience RJ report enhanced ability to understand peers, manage emotions, feel greater empathy, resolve conflict with parents, improve their home environment, and maintain positive relationships with peers. They are learning life skills and sustainable conflict management skills. Throughout the district, more than 88% of teachers reported that RJ was very or somewhat helpful in managing difficult student behaviors in the classroom (Jain, Bassey, Brown, & Kalra, 2014).

In Oakland and several other districts throughout the United States, RJ is implemented through a three-tier, school-wide model.

Tier 1: Community Building (Prevent/Relate). Tier 1 is characterized by the use of SEL skills and practice (classroom circles) to build relationships, create shared values and guidelines, and promote restorative conversations following behavioral disruption. The goal is to build a caring, intentional, and equitable community to help create conditions for learning.

Tier 2: Restorative Processes (Intervene/Repair). Tier 2 is characterized by the use of nonpunitive response to harm or conflict such as harm circles, mediation, or family-group conferencing to respond to disciplinary issues in a restorative manner. This process addresses the root causes of the harm, supports accountability for the offender, and promotes healing for the victim(s), the offender, and the school community.

Tier 3: Supported Reentry (Individualize/Reintegrate). Tier 3 is characterized by one-on-one support and successful reentry of youth following suspension, truancy, expulsion, or incarceration. The goal is to welcome youth to the school community in a manner that provides wraparound support and promotes student accountability and achievement. (Jain et al., 2014)

Similar to mindfulness, RJ is a growing field, and a number of helpful resources are readily available to become trained in RJ. If you plan to implement RJ in any way in your classroom, I highly recommend you seek out training, especially if you would like to engage in Tier 2 or Tier 3 RJ. What follows is a small slice of a few key practices inspired by RJ, which can be easily implemented in your classroom to help create conditions for learning, foster a positive climate, and build relationships.

Practice: Community-Building Circles to Create Class Agreements

RJ is more of a philosophy than a curriculum. I engage in community circles during the first week of school and then monthly. Since I've started incorporating community circles into my teaching practice, I've seen a drastic reduction in referrals and conflicts between students. It doesn't go away 100%, but circle practice builds a more cohesive community. When teachers signal to students there are opportunities to talk about things, and teachers can let go and use a talking piece to let students speak, it builds trust.

—James Barbuto, Skyline High School social studies
teacher and codirector of the Education Academy

One of the most important practices teachers can engage in is to coconstruct classroom agreements with their students. Doing this offers transparency and collectively agreed-upon expectations around in-class behavior and interactions. Most importantly, it creates an opportunity for students to be authentic stakeholders in the classroom environment that they helped create. A community-building circle can be a powerful structure to facilitate the coconstruction of classroom agreements.

Sitting in a circle feels markedly different from sitting in rows. When you are in rows, there's an inherent power dynamic with everyone facing forward, facing a leader. When you sit in a circle, you experience a stronger sense of community; there's a sense of connection and shared responsibility. Circles frequently use an object called a talking piece during a session to make it clear who has the right to speak. The talking piece can be anything that is easily passed from one student to another and is utilized to promote equity of voice. The circle also has a center, and this is an important element. While it can be left clear, it's powerful to place something in the center. Students can take turns preparing the center of the circle. In several classrooms of teachers I work with, students alternate the role of circle keeper. The circle keeper is responsible for facilitating the circle process, crafting high-quality prompts for discussion, and preparing the center of the circle. Oftentimes I've seen plants in the center, special stones, or even cultural artifacts that are meaningful to some students.

At the start of the school year when you are especially trying to create a sense of trust in your classroom, engaging in a circle process with low-risk prompts can be a great way to have your students get to know each other and begin to build a sense of community and connection. I highly recommend the book *Circle Forward* (Boyes-Watson & Pranis, 2014) to help you get started with incorporating community-building circles into your classroom.

Here are common guidelines for engaging in a community-building circle. When sharing these guidelines with students, invite them to define what each guideline means to them.

- Respect the talking piece.
- Speak from the heart.
- Listen from the heart.
- No need to rehearse.
- Without feeling rushed, say just enough.
- Right to pass.

After introducing the circle guidelines, invite students to generate additional guidelines to follow when they are in circle. To help build consensus around the additional guidelines, have students utilize a consensus-building tool like "fists to five" or "thumbs up, thumbs down, thumbs sideways." Fists to five is a simple strategy for building consensus. Each person votes by holding up zero, one, two, three, four, or five fingers, and the circle keeper looks around the circle to tally votes. Zero fingers (a fist): I will not go along with it—a way to block consensus. One finger: I have serious reservations about this idea. While I vote to move forward, I'd prefer to resolve the concerns before supporting it. Two fingers: I have some concerns, but I'll go along and try it. Three fingers: I will support the idea. Four fingers: I like this idea, sounds good. Five fingers: Absolutely, best idea ever! I'll champion it. Anyone with a fist or one finger is invited to speak and share why they feel the way they do. Thumbs up, thumbs down, thumbs sideways is often used to support student self-assessment in the classroom, but it can also be used as a consensus-building strategy, and adapting it in this way signals that a thumbs up supports the idea, sideways thumb suggests the participant is neutral and can accept the idea, and thumbs down suggests the participant is not in support of the idea. Those who are not in full agreement are often invited to speak and share why.

Once circle guidelines are established, you can then engage students around coconstructing class agreements. Depending on how much time you have, teachers may offer an initial list of possible agreements and, utilizing the talking piece, have students revise or build upon this list. Some teachers choose to have students weigh in on classroom expectations and present the expectations as what the entire class, including the teacher, intends to follow along with developing consequences.

CIRCLE PLANNING GUIDE FOR COCONSTRUCTING
CLASSROOM AGREEMENTS

Purpose of the Circle: What's your purpose, goal, or intended outcome for the circle?

To coconstruct classroom agreements and create a space for dialogue, discussion, and student voice around how our class intends to be with each other this year.

Circle Introduction: How do you plan to introduce the focus for the circle?

As a classroom community, it's important for us to take time to reflect and collectively coconstruct and agree upon expectations around in-class behavior and interactions. Doing this creates an opportunity for all of us to be authentic stakeholders in the classroom environment we've all helped to create.

Circle Guidelines: What are some guidelines you would like to introduce from the start? How will you invite participants to provide input on these guidelines and offer additional ones? How will you document the guidelines?

Offer common guidelines for engaging in a community-building circle (e.g., respect the talking piece; speak from the heart; listen from the heart; no need to rehearse; without feeling rushed, say just enough, right to pass).

When sharing these guidelines with students, invite them to define what each guideline means to them. Then invite students to generate additional guidelines to follow in circle and engage in a consensus-building strategy.

Record agreed-upon guidelines on poster paper and have each student sign, demonstrating collective agreement.

Opening: How do you plan to open the circle? Mindful breathing, story, music, song, quote?

Sound a chime or a bell of mindfulness and have students gently bring awareness to their breathing. Guide students to place a hand on either their heart, chest, or abdomen and pay attention to their inhales and exhales. With each breath, students can also silently say a word or phrase that provides them with some comfort, such as "peace" or "joy."

Introduce Talking Piece: What object are you using for a talking piece and why?

Share what you chose for a talking piece and why; then remind students of the talking piece guidelines and the purpose for using a talking piece (to promote equity of voice).

Check-In: What question will you ask for the initial check-in round?

Ask students to first reflect on a positive learning experience and environment (either in or out of school) and have students share one to three conditions that made that learning experience work for them. Other questions could include "What helps your learning?" or "What hinders your learning?" or "What does learning look like, sound like, and feel like to you?"

Discussion: What will you address in the circle? How many rounds do you anticipate facilitating? (When planning this portion of the circle process, try to anticipate some challenges that may occur and how you may handle them.)

Remind students back into the purpose of the circle (to coconstruct agreements for the classroom community) and engage in the following rounds of questions:
- Round 1: What do we value? For example, respect, kindness, honoring commitments, etc.
- Round 2: Based on what you named as a value, how would we need to be with each other to honor that value? For example, we value education so we create a place where everyone can learn without being disturbed.
- Round 3: For each value action statement offered in Round 2, get specific. For example, what does it mean to create a place where everyone can learn without being disturbed? What would that look like in terms of agreed-upon behavior and actions?
- Round 4: Utilize a consensus-building strategy for the class agreements.

Check Out: What question do you want to ask to bring some sense of closure to this circle?

How do we ensure that these agreements are lived? What can we suggest for revisiting our agreements and revising if needed? How do we hold ourselves accountable to what we just created?

Closing: How do you want to close the circle? Breathing, quote, story, poem, and so on.

Open the circle up for one final round of appreciations. Invite each student to appreciate someone or some aspect of the circle you all just experienced together. If time permits, you can also invite them to share how they feel now compared to how they felt at the start of the class and detail why.

To further support student ownership of the class agreements, invite student volunteers to create a visual representation of the agreements on a large poster. This can then hang in a prominent place where the class can continually refer to it (preferably near the circle guidelines students signed).

I can't stress enough that in order for the agreements to be lived and not merely laminated, teachers must continually revisit them. Ideally, agreements are revisited in every class using a simple prompt: *"In class today, focus in on one of our agreements that you'd like to pay special attention to."* Then, at the end of class and if possible periodically throughout class, *"Come back to the classroom community agreement you are focusing on today. How are we doing on it? Share your thoughts with the person sitting next to you."*

Creating a shared sense of agreements also sets the stage for a restorative, rather than punitive, approach if a discipline issue arises. For example, when responding to conflict, you can employ a restorative approach by asking those involved the following key questions:

1. What happened, and what were you thinking at the time of the incident?
2. What have you thought about since?
3. Who has been affected by what happened, and how?
4. What about this has been the hardest for you?
5. What do you think needs to be done to make things as right as possible?

If you have a shared set of class agreements that all students have bought into, it makes it much easier to engage in the restorative process. Through engaging in these questions, you focus on the harm done rather than the rule itself, which helps strengthen and restore relationships. Restorative practices also build capacity around a student's self-management, a critical life skill and one of the five SEL core competencies.

Practice: Making the SEL Competencies Explicit in Circle Practice

If you are interested in making the SEL competencies an explicit part of circle practice, here's a sample lesson plan you can utilize with your students.

CIRCLE PLANNING GUIDE FOR INTRODUCING SEL

Purpose of the Circle: What's your purpose, goal or intended outcome for the circle?

Students use the circle process to build community and learn about the five social and emotional learning competencies.

Classroom Setup

Before class, place chairs in a circle. Students sit in a circle to promote a sense of equality. Preferably, there are no tables or obtrusive objects inside the circle so that participants are open to each other.

Centerpiece: The centerpiece is a shared space in the middle of the circle. The centerpiece may include decorative materials such as cloth, plants, guidelines, values, or symbolic items.

Talking piece: The talking piece is an object used to facilitate conversation that is often symbolic to the circle keeper. (The circle keeper poses a question or activity for the participants and then passes the talking piece around the circle. Each participant has equal opportunity to participate or pass. Only the person holding the talking piece may speak or act while all others listen respectfully.)

Circle Introduction: How do you plan to introduce the focus for the circle?

Explain that today they will experience the circle process, which is based in the wisdom and practices found in indigenous cultures around the world. As a community, they will have an opportunity to reflect on what social and emotional learning is and what it means for us.

Circle Guidelines: What are some guidelines you would like to introduce? How will you invite participants to provide input on these guidelines and offer additional ones? How will you document the guidelines?

Going around the circle in order, passing the talking piece from one student to the next, ask each student to offer a condition for how students must interact and behave so all students can speak honestly and respectfully. For example, "How would you like to see each of us in our circle treat each other during this conversation?"

Record student responses on a poster-sized sheet of paper, which you will have all students sign after they provide input. These are now your circle agreements for the rest of the year.

Opening: How do you plan to open the circle? Mindful breathing, story, music, song, quote?

Sound a bell of mindfulness and have students gently bring awareness to their breathing. Guide students to place a hand on either their heart, chest, or abdomen and pay attention to their inhales and exhales. With each breath, students can also silently say a word or phrase that provides them with some comfort, such as "peace" or "joy."

Introduce Talking Piece: What object are you using for a talking piece and why?

Share what you chose for a talking piece and why; then remind students of the talking piece guidelines and the purpose for using a talking piece (to promote equity of voice).

Check-In: What question will you ask for the initial check-in round?

Have the definition of social and emotional learning posted in the room or create a handout for each student with the definition. Feel free to use your school, district, or state's definition of SEL. Ask for a volunteer to read the definition:

Social and emotional learning (SEL) is a process through which children and adults develop the fundamental skills for life effectiveness. These are the skills we all need to handle ourselves, our relationships, and our work effectively and ethically. We believe everyone strengthening their social-emotional skills and competencies enhances our ability to connect across race, class, culture, language, gender, gender identity, sexual orientation, learning needs, and age. (Oakland Unified School District SEL Definition)

Ask students what they think the definition means. At the end of this round, share with students that we hope to exercise these SEL competencies in every class.

Activity and Discussion: What will you address in the circle? How many rounds do you anticipate facilitating? (When planning this portion of the circle process, try to anticipate some challenges that may occur and plan how you may handle them.)

Invite students to complete the self-assessment on SEL I Statements on the bottom half of the student handout. They are to mark a star (*) next to any statement they feel they practice really well, a check (✔) next to any statements they feel proficient at, and a delta (Δ) next to any statements they feel they need to work on.

SEL I Statements

(These SEL I Statements were coconstructed with students and adults in the Oakland Unified School District.)

Self-Awareness

I am fully aware of who I am culturally, socially, emotionally and physically.

Self-Management

I manage my thoughts, feelings, and actions to help me work toward a better me within my home, my school, and my community.

Social Awareness

I understand, respect, and value the perspective of people who are like me and different from me.

Relationship Skills

I can communicate effectively to make and keep healthy relationships with diverse individuals.

Responsible Decision-Making

I make decisions that are ethical and safe, and consider the well-being of myself and others.

I have the knowledge and skills that I need to make healthy choices for myself and to advocate for the health of others.

Overarching

I can explain how I use the SEL skills and competencies in my life and their impact on me being prepared for college, career, and community.

After students engage in this activity, go around in a circle and have students share how they use the SEL skills and competencies in their life and their impact on being prepared for college, career, and community.

Or ask, why is SEL important for learning and life?

Check Out: What question do you want to ask to bring some sense of closure to this circle?

Ask students to choose one of the five SEL competencies to intentionally practice, name it to the group, and explain why they chose that competency and how they will practice it.

Closing: How do you want to close the circle? Breathing, quote, story, poem, etc.

Share with students that we will close with practicing our SEL self-awareness and self-management skills through mindful breathing. Invite a bell of mindfulness and have students gently focus on the rise and fall of their breathing.

In addition to explicitly naming SEL in the circle practice, the circle process itself can provide a venue for learning about and practicing our SEL skills. Here are some ways the circle process directly connects to the five core SEL competencies:

- **Self-Awareness:** Circle creates a safe space to explore and appreciate identity and diversity, and to share personal and cultural values.
- **Self-Management:** Circle participants establish shared guidelines and practice monitoring and managing emotions and behaviors to reach the goals of the group. The use of a talking piece provides an opportunity to practice patience and self-regulation.
- **Social Awareness:** Sharing personal stories and listening to the stories of others allows peers to experience empathy and build understanding and respect for others.
- **Relationship Skills:** Circle relies upon building strong community relationships, allows for collaborative decision making, and provides a process for effectively responding to conflict and harm.
- **Responsible Decision-Making:** Circle brings people together to be accountable for personal choices and behavior and to have the opportunity to learn and choose how to repair harm caused to individuals and the community.

Adapted from Oakland Unified School District Peer RJ Guide

If you'd like to go deeper in your introduction of SEL through the circle process or want to use questions to help build student understanding of the competencies, you can utilize the following simple definitions for each competency and the question prompts. You can then revisit the questions in your daily lessons as you make SEL explicit in your academic instruction.

Self-Awareness

I understand who I am, and how my feelings about myself and others influence my actions. I know my strengths and opportunities for growth. I know when I need help and how to get help.

- What am I good at and how do I know?
- When I don't understand something or need help, what do I do?
- What am I feeling right now and how can I act in a way that is helpful for myself and others?

Self-Management

I express my feelings and handle my actions in skillful ways. I set goals and I achieve them.

- What goals have I set for myself? How will I achieve my goals?
- What do I do when things get in the way of achieving my goals?
- How can I share my feelings in ways that are helpful to myself and respectful to others?

Social Awareness

I care about and work with people like me and people different from me. I understand and respect their thoughts, feelings, and points of view.

- What do I do to work well with people like me and people different from me?
- How can I understand others and respect where they are coming from?
- What am I doing to make my school community a better place?

Relationship Skills

I interact in ways that build positive relationships with people like me and different from me. I am able to handle conflicts in healthy ways.

- What skills do I have for getting along well with others?
- How do I work with people who are like me and different from me?
- How do I listen and express myself to keep healthy relationships?

Responsible Decision-Making

I act in ways that are respectful and safe. I consider how my choices and decisions will affect myself and others.

- What steps do I take to know that I am making a skillful choice?

- How will this decision affect myself and others?
- How do I accept the outcomes of my choices?

(These SEL statements and questions were developed by the Oakland Unified School District SEL Team for use in SEL posters distributed throughout our school district.)

Schools that are fully committed to implementing RJ usually have a staff member that has received substantial training, who then builds the capacity of all teachers to engage in Tier 1 community-building circles. Oftentimes these schools devote the first four to six weeks of the school year to building a positive culture and climate through the use of circle practice. Some teachers are then able to hold circles every other week to help sustain community and check in with students.

Investing this amount of time in community building may be challenging for secondary teachers given curricular demands. Still, even spending the first few days of school engaged in circle practice and coconstructing agreements can then set the tone for the rest of the year as long as there are opportunities to deepen community through teaching practices like academic discussion. For example, several teachers who engage in community-building circles take elements of RJ and apply them to academic contexts. One popular practice is to utilize the circle structure and talking pieces when students are engaged in academic discussion or any type of class discussion until the skills needed to engage in classroom conversations become more fluid.

There are also many other ways teachers can individually connect with each student daily so they feel more seen. A few years ago a video on *Good Morning America* went viral, in which teacher Barry White Jr. of Charlotte, North Carolina, greeted each of his students with special hand-shakes every day before they entered class. It's well worth watching. This was a simple yet powerful way to recognize each student individually on a daily basis.

Skillful Self-Disclosure

Students learn as much for a teacher as from a teacher.

—Linda Darling-Hammond

Another way to build trust with students is to engage in skillful self-disclosure. In the field of business there is evidence that leaders who show up as their authentic selves can not only build trust but generate greater cooperation and teamwork as well (Offermann & Rosh, 2012). In order to create an authentic relationship with adolescents, they need to know you are a human being. "Skillful" is the key word here. Used incorrectly, this practice can backfire, and it's important to disclose just enough to connect with students, but not too much.

One example of an appropriate practice I have employed in the class-room at the start of the year is a letter I wrote to my students sharing about where I grew up, what my family and cultural background is, where I went to college, what I studied, learning challenges I've had, and how I overcame them. I also shared personal passions and hobbies, music and art that inspired me, and why I decided to become a teacher. This letter modeled what I then expected of students in a letter to me. Once I received these letters from my students, I then wrote a personal response to each of them. This did take a lot of time because teaching middle or high school I had many students, but it made a real difference when students received a personal response where I would acknowledge what they shared in their letter to me and communicate connections I and the student might have. Taking the time and effort to do this at the start of the school year not only helped establish a positive individual relationship with each student, but it also informed me about any learning challenges students might have and how I could help them.

Supporting All Learners

A great way to create a supportive learning community is to have students engage in an activity that normalizes having learning challenges. Start off by sharing a learning challenge you have and the ways in which you sought support. Then have students anonymously detail their specific learning challenges on pieces of paper. Collect the papers and chart what students wrote. To create safety and preserve anonymity, it is best not to have a student do the charting in case someone recognizes another student's handwriting. Have students group the learning challenges and then as a class go through strategies for each learning challenge and make agreements for how you will support each other. Post this chart with strategies and agreements of support in the class and refer to it when you introduce new lessons or assignments. Revisit the chart and make additions or changes, and add strategies throughout the year.

Sustaining Community:
The Three Signature SEL Practices

One strength of the SEL signature practices is their simplicity and repeatability; consistently used, they can sustain a steady music of engagement.
> —Mike Jones, English teacher and SEL lead teacher, Oakland High School

Once you've invested time in building a sense of community in your classroom, it's important to incorporate practices that help sustain community. The three signature SEL practices were developed by my mentor and colleague, CASEL professional development consultant Ann McKay Bryson. These practices are used widely among classroom teachers to sustain community while also promoting academic engagement (Engaging Schools defines academic engagement as "sustained learning that involves students emotionally, cognitively, and behaviorally"). When I lead SEL professional learning engagements for middle and high school teachers, participants consistently cite these practices as their most important takeaway:

1. Welcoming routines and rituals (activities for inclusion)
2. Engaging pedagogy (academic integration, transitions, brain breaks)
3. Optimistic closure (reflections and looking forward)

When used consistently, these three SEL practices can create conditions for growth and learning across all five SEL competencies while simultaneously using culturally responsive teaching strategies that highlight relationality and student voice.

The two key components when designing a welcoming ritual, incorporating engaging pedagogy, or utilizing optimistic closure are individual time for reflection and intentional social interaction. These elements are critical because research has consistently shown that time for reflection results in significant benefits to student learning (Bennett, 2016), including an increased number of student responses. Thoughtfully designed social interactions support structured collaborative learning experiences, which result in student achievement gains, as several studies have shown (Dean, Hubbell, Pitler, & Stone, 2012). Additionally, engaging practices including brain breaks in particular emphasize a powerful strategy that the organization Engaging Schools developed called 30, 90, 10. This refers to having students move every 30 minutes for 90 seconds, 10 feet if possible.

Consistency when incorporating these practices is key. Schools provide an important opportunity for rewiring the neural pathways necessary for habits to be built and sustained. Dr. Richard Davidson, a neuroscientist at the University of Wisconsin, speaks about how every behavioral intervention is also a biological intervention (2015). Building on this, Ann McKay Bryson shares:

> Having routines and rituals in our classrooms and school communities is beneficial for every child, and absolutely critical for some. Through offering repetitive and engaging opportunities, these foundational strategies help students improve the skills and habits of self-awareness and social awareness through noticing and naming feelings, and seeing how they are connected to what is happening within us and around us. These practices also promote self-management and relationship skills by interacting with people and with content in ways that intentionally strengthen our skill set of being aware and in control of our thoughts, emotions, actions and interactions. When well-developed, these skills lead to responsible decision making in school and in life.

The table below offers some examples of these strategies and in the Recommended Resources section I've provided the names of additional books that contain more examples of these practices. When designing your lesson plan, it's important to change it up. McKay Bryson suggests balancing newness within routines and rituals because, while our brains are often calmed by sameness, they need freshness too.

Welcoming Rituals (2–10 minutes)	**Examples From the Classroom**
Activities for Inclusion	• Every voice is heard
	• Purposeful social interactions
Ritual openings establish safety and predictability, support contribution by all voices, reinforce norms for respectful listening, allow students to connect with one another, and create a sense of belonging. To be successful, these activities must be carefully chosen, connected to the learning of the day, and engagingly facilitated.	• Class meetings
	• Smile and greet each person by name
	Schoolwide
	• Adults express joy in seeing students
	• Stack of breakfast items on office counter expresses gladness to see late arrivals
	• Morning announcements include student voice
Engaging Practices (1–15 minutes)	**Examples From the Classroom**
Academic Integration, Sense Making, Transitions, and Brain Breaks	• Opportunities for interaction: Cultivate practices that involve interactions in partnerships, triads, small groups, and as a whole group
Engaging practices are brain-compatible strategies that can foster relationships, cultural humility and responsiveness, empowerment, and collaboration. Intentionally build student SEL skills and then authentically practice these skills throughout the school day. Provide thoughtful transitions and opportunities for brain breaks that help integrate new information into long-term memory, otherwise it is soon forgotten. Balance opportunities for quiet reflection and writing with more active activities.	• Explicitly teach SEL skills
	• Turn to your partner: Sharing and listening to make sense of new input
	• Cocreate and regularly revisit working agreements with your students
	• Brain Break, Stand and Stretch: Refresh and reset the brain with movement, music, quiet reflection

Optimistic Closings (3–5 minutes) Reflections and Looking Forward	Examples From the Classroom
Provide intentional closure by having students reflect on and then name something that helps them transition on an optimistic note. This provides a positive way to reinforce learning, can connect school to home and community, and creates a moment of looking forward to coming back.	Think of . . . • Something I learned today • Someone I was able to help • Something I want to share with an adult • Something I'm looking forward to doing tomorrow • Something I enjoyed about the day • Someone who was kind or helpful to me

(Adapted from Oakland Unified School District SEL Team and the work of Ann McKay Bryson, CASEL professional development consultant)

In Chapter 4, these three practices are incorporated into a lesson planning template that supports making SEL more intentional and explicit in daily instruction. McKay Bryson affirms that when the three signature SEL practices are "carefully chosen, effectively facilitated, and thoughtfully debriefed, they contribute to building a sense of connection, consistency, and community." For example, in Summit Preparatory Charter High School in Redwood City, California, Aukeem Ballard has his students engage in an optimistic closing called Appreciation, Apology, Aha, where students share an appreciation, apology, or insight with their class. Students share things like, "I apologize for having my headphones on," or "I would like to thank everyone for taking this class seriously." Ballard invites students to share what they genuinely think will be useful for people to hear. He also has students snap, clap, or show with their hands when they hear something they agree or connect with.

"When you pay attention to each other, not only does it build a sense of community, but we're more able to understand other people," says Janet, a 12th-grade student. "If you're able to understand people at a younger age, you could work better with them as adults. That changes how the future generations will be. People can be more accepting, more helpful towards each other" (George Lucas Educational Foundation, 2018).

Note From the Field

Oftentimes when schools and districts take on social and emotional learning, they focus primarily on SEL standards or indicators for students only, as if adults have already mastered all aspects of SEL. We know of course that this is not true. In Oakland, our standards are actually pre-K–adult, and there is a strong belief that SEL is for adults as much as it is for young people. A few years ago when we began to build out developmental indicators for our SEL standards, we engaged high school youth in building out what the five core SEL competencies looked like and sounded like for teachers. For example, if a teacher is socially aware, how does that manifest in the classroom? How might you engage your students around what SEL looks like and sounds like for teachers? Take it even further and reflect on how you may engage parents and the community in a conversation around what SEL looks like for adults.

Starting Where You Are

To achieve greatness, start where you are, use what you have, do what you can.
—Arthur Ashe

In this chapter, you were introduced to a few key practices that can help create the conditions for having a relationship-centered classroom. While the practices presented in this chapter are certainly not an exhaustive list, they can be a good starting point. The key is to remember that creating community starts with you. When we fly, we are reminded (in time of emergency) to always put our oxygen masks on first before assisting our children. Similarly, we cannot create a positive climate in our classroom unless we first attend to creating a positive climate within ourselves.

Explore which practices really resonate with you from this chapter and choose one to implement consistently. Find a teaching buddy who is also interested in having a more relationship-centered classroom and find ways to check in with and support each other.

SEL Teaching Practices and Integration With Common Core

We have to bust the false binary that suggests we must choose between an academically rigorous pedagogy and one geared toward social justice.

—Jeff Duncan Andrade

Integrating SEL with academic learning happens through what students learn (the curriculum) and how they learn it (the process). This chapter provides guidance on teaching practices, like the one described below, that infuse and reinforce SEL while also providing opportunities to teach SEL skills explicitly. I also explore the connection between SEL and project-based learning, Common Core, personalized learning, and how SEL is integral to successful high school improvement strategies like Linked Learning.

MIDDLE SCHOOL HUMANITIES TEACHERS

Common Core allows for teaching more radical things because it is skill-based versus content-based so you can frame a lot of what's taught around helping students become better readers, writers, and communicators versus knowing where Mesopotamia is. I think geography has a value in and of itself, but developing our students as critical thinkers and effective communicators outweighs simply learning dry facts.

If schools want to ensure that students regardless of circumstance can further their schooling and use the language of power, then teaching students how to express themselves effectively must be prioritized. In the United States, our race and class affect our access to opportunities and how we experience the world. Instructional practices like academic discussion help students develop their SEL skills through learning how to engage in active listening, respecting the speaker, paraphrasing, and asking clarifying questions to make sure you understand what is being said.

You can't just expect that students will know how to engage in academic discussion. The scaffolding I set up to create the conditions for students to participate effectively was thought through carefully ahead of time. For example, we started out by really examining what it means to agree and what it means to disagree and explored the difference between a clarifying question and a probing question. We spent time detailing what each move in academic discussion looks like and sounds like, emphasizing that the most important thing is caring about understanding your partner.

Morgan Kirschbaum,
Edna Brewer Middle School, Oakland, CA

SEL Teaching Practices

My teacher education program, like so many others, filled me with a lot of theory but lacked the practical guidance I needed in order to create structures to promote learning in my classroom. In Chapter 2, we were introduced to the three signature SEL practices, one of which was engaging practices, which I like to think of as the "how" of teaching. Engaging practices are infused with SEL, vary in complexity, and consist of sequential steps facilitated by the teacher to support learning individually and collectively, like the use of "turn to your partner," "Socratic seminar," or "jigsaw." Since SEL is implicit in engaging practices, it's critical that as teachers we do the work of making SEL explicit if we want to truly engage in SEL integrated instruction. The way we do this is to reflect on the SEL skills needed and utilized in the engaging practice. As we detail the steps of the practice in our lesson planning, we must look for opportunities to make sure we are also explicitly teaching those SEL skills, much like Morgan did by having his students detail what each move in academic discussion looked like and sounded like at the start of this chapter.

In order to reinforce these SEL skills, it's important that students reflect on not just their academic learning but also how they did with practicing their SEL skills. In 2014, American Institutes for Research's Nick Yoder published a research-to-practice brief that identified 10 teaching practices that promote SEL. What follows are deeper dives into four of those high-impact teaching practices that can be used across grade level and content areas to develop SEL skills and support academic learning in secondary classrooms.

- Academic discussion
- Cooperative learning
- Self-reflection and self-assessment
- Student voice and choice

A note here about technology. While it is true that technology is impacting the way we learn since we now have the capacity to learn anything as long as we have a device to connect to the internet and a connection, the skills students learn and practice in the following teaching practices are timeless because they are the same skills employers cite as being most critical. For example, my brother-in-law, who works for Google, shared with me that one of the key traits in being hired is "googlyness," which essentially means how well one can work in a team. Working successfully in teams requires a tremendous amount of SEL. If our job as secondary teachers is preparing our students for life success, then we need to equip them with the SEL skills needed to cultivate positive professional and personal relationships.

Once when I was leading training, I asked participants where they learned SEL. One woman stood up and said, "I learned SEL in my three marriages—I mean divorces." Everyone laughed, but her statement was poignant. These are also the skills we need in order to have effective human relationships, which are so key to our overall happiness and well-being. I often joke that my SEL skills really deepened only when I got married! SEL is a lifelong process, and the more we practice, the better we get.

Academic Discussion

Academic discussion refers to classroom conversations that promote critical thinking and deepen understanding of academic content. There are several engaging practices that can support academic discussion through structured interaction, and teachers play a critical role in asking open-ended questions and having students explain their thinking and build on their classmates' thinking. Successful academic discussion can happen only when the class has collectively defined expectations, and students have had enough time and support to effectively engage with the content being discussed so they can reference textual evidence.

Features of Effective Discussion Tasks

1. Require both partners to talk.

2. Require critical and creative thinking.

3. Take advantage of controversies and conflict.

4. Recognize and reduce ambiguity.

5. Encourage thinking based on principles, laws, and approaches of the discipline.

6. Build in opportunities for transfer of knowledge and skills.

7. Provide choice and ownership.

Developing Discussion Prompts Checklist

Does the prompt leave room for multiple perspectives or solutions? Is the prompt open ended? Does the prompt connect to a big idea or essential question of the lesson or unit? Is the prompt engaging to students? Is it worthy of discussion? Does the prompt require students to think critically? Is the prompt posted?

(Zwiers & Crawford, 2011)

How Academic Discussion Promotes SEL

Academic discussion can support student SEL development in a number of ways. Below is a chart developed in the Oakland Unified School District that combines our SEL anchor standards with classroom indicator examples.

SEL COMPETENCY	CLASSROOM INDICATOR EXAMPLE
Self-Awareness: What are you good at in this class and how do you know you are good at it? When you don't understand something in this class, what do you do?	
Develop and demonstrate self-awareness skills to: • Identify personal, cultural, and linguistic assets • Identify prejudices and biases toward people different than oneself • Understand the connections between one's emotions, social contexts, and identity • Demonstrate an accurate self-concept based on one's strengths and challenges • Identify when help is needed and who can provide it	Students: • Reflect on their progress as a learner • Express what is easy or hard about the academic discussion and why • Ask for help when needed • Identify their role and responsibilities during academic discussions
Self-Management: How do you move toward your goal, especially when you lose focus or are stuck or stressed?	
Develop and demonstrate self-management skills to: • Regulate one's emotions and behaviors in contexts with people different than oneself • Motivate oneself to set and achieve goals	Students: • Manage and express emotions and thoughts in a constructive way • Stay engaged in discussion • Use I messages in the social context of academic discussion

SEL COMPETENCY	CLASSROOM INDICATOR EXAMPLE
Social Awareness: When you are working in a group, how do you make sure it's fair for everyone?	
Develop and demonstrate social awareness skills to: • Establish and maintain healthy interactions and relationships across diverse communities • Embrace diversity and take the perspectives of people different from oneself • Demonstrate empathy for people similar to and different from oneself	Students: • Listen attentively to others' ideas • Respectfully paraphrase others' ideas • Engage collaboratively with people different from oneself • Able to take the perspective of people different from oneself • Add to and build on others' ideas
Relationship Skills: What do you do so that your classmates and teacher have heard and understand your ideas and what you are saying?	
Develop and demonstrate relationship skills to: • Relate to people similar to and different than oneself • Communicate clearly and effectively • Build, establish, and maintain healthy relationships	Students: • Communicate clearly and effectively with people different from oneself • Engage in constructive argument • Give and receive constructive feedback • Listen, encourage, acknowledge, compromise, work toward consensus • Express value of collaboration • Ask questions based on careful listening

SEL COMPETENCY	CLASSROOM INDICATOR EXAMPLE
Responsible Decision-Making: When you are working with others, how do you make a decision?	
Develop and demonstrate responsible decision-making skills to: • Problem solve effectively while being respectful of people similar to and different from oneself • Behave responsibly in personal, professional, and community contexts • Make constructive and respectful choices that consider the well-being of self and others	Students: • Follow norms established for the discussion • Actively participate in group decision-making process • Generate alternative ideas and solutions • Demonstrate the good of the group • Ask why and what-if questions

Suggestions for Making SEL Explicit

When designing the prompts for academic discussion, what SEL connections can you make? For example, as students analyze one of the characters in a story, they can also reflect on the emotional life of the character and deepen their emotional literacy through utilizing a feelings chart. Or when they utilize the claims, evidence, reasoning framework in science, they can also evaluate the impact of stress on the brain and reflect on stress management strategies. Academic discussion also has thinking focuses that can connect to SEL competencies. Discussions that center on cause and effect or problem solving could be opportunities to explore responsible decision making. Analyzing a character or making a claim can connect with social awareness. Prompts that elicit self-reflection are a chance to practice self-awareness.

When structuring interaction (think-pair-share, Socratic seminar, etc.) identify the specific SEL skills (e.g., perspective taking, relationship building) you want your students to focus on, how you will emphasize that, and how you and your students will ensure equitable participation (e.g., use of a talking piece initially until students have strengthened their communication skills enough to have a more fluid, respectful conversation where everyone contributes).

When introducing academic discussion, have students detail the SEL skills needed for academic discussion and discuss what each skill looks like and sounds like. From this, collectively create an SEL academic discussion participation protocol. Students can use this to self-assess, and you can use it to assess your students too.

Students need a lot of training and practice to successfully engage in academic discussion. Having students utilize a discussion prep sheet where SEL is made explicit can be useful. The following academic discussion SEL reflection on page 90 was first introduced to me by my SEL counterparts in the Washoe County School District:

GOING DEEPER

In her 11th grade English class at Fremont High School in Oakland, California, Agnes Zapata wanted to improve accountability in small-group discussions. She recognized the value of small-group discussions because her students often felt safer in smaller groups and had more opportunities to speak than they would in a large class, but

SEL SKILLS NEEDED FOR ACADEMIC DISCUSSION: QUESTIONS FOR STUDENTS

Name: _____

Text: _____

What SEL skills do I plan to focus on? What is my SEL intention for this academic discussion?

_____

Questions for Academic Discussion:

On a scale of 1–5 (5 being great), I rate my attention to my SEL focus area and intention a __
 because _____

_____

Which of the following is an area you want to focus on in our next discussion? Circle and explain your choice.

- Listening attentively to others
- Staying focused on the point of the discussion
- Articulating your own thoughts clearly and concisely
- Responding directly to other students' points
- Asking probing questions
- Other: _____

What strategies will you use to improve in the focus area you've chosen for our next discussion?

_____

What's an interesting or new idea presented in our discussion?

_____

What quote from the text or discussion do you most want to remember? Why?

_____

given her class size she wasn't always able to hear every student's contribution. Instead of having a recorder write what each small group discussed, she decided to have her students use the technology they already had. She said that having students use their cell phones to record their small-group conversations and then send the recording to her cut down on talking off-topic, inappropriate language, or moments of silence. Students used the phone much like passing the mic, and classmates held each other accountable because they were trusting the group member with the phone to be the recorder.

This practice was able to work because Agnes spent time at the start of the year coconstructing agreements with students that included skillful use of technology. When discussing technology with students, it's helpful for them to explore how they can use technology instead of having the technology use them.

Cooperative Learning

I have found that social-emotional learning skills embedded into the curriculum plus cooperative learning structures plus reflection equal optimum lifelong learning. There is power in the embedded curriculum. Many students learn better when the skill is applied.

—Stephanie Knight

Cooperation means working together to achieve shared goals. Cooperative learning involves more than just putting students in groups and instructing them to work together. Cooperative learning has to be taught, and SEL is essential. Cooperative learning consists of five key ingredients (Johnson et al., 2006):

1. *Positive interdependence* is the belief that all group members feel that each person's effort benefits all group members. Having clear roles and responsibilities within the group, along with a shared goal and system of accountability, can promote depending on each other.

2. *Individual accountability* occurs when an "individual public performance is required" (Kagan, 2011). In other words, cooperative learning must involve elements that each student performs on their own, this performance is seen by someone else, and it is compulsory.

3. *Promoting one another's successes* requires that students are personally committed to each other and their mutual goals. This happens through positive interactions where students actively advance each other's learning.

4. *Applying interpersonal and social skills* involves learning academic content and SEL skills simultaneously. Groups must have relationship skills, make responsible decisions, and practice self and social awareness and self-manage.

5. *Group processing* happens when the group reflects and discusses their progress toward the lesson's goal.

A few years ago I was working with a teacher who was dedicated to integrating SEL into all of her classes. One of the ways she sought to do this was through implementing cooperative learning, but she didn't utilize any structures to support students in working in groups. In one of my early coaching sessions, I had her watch a short video clip I took of her students attempting to work together, and it was clear that they didn't know how to work together or even that they needed to work together. I introduced her to the five key ingredients and various group learning protocols. Once she designed her lessons paying special attention to all of the aspects of cooperative learning, her students were much more on task and engaged, and the quality of their work improved accordingly.

How Cooperative Learning Promotes SEL

Cooperative learning offers an opportunity for students to learn and practice all five SEL competencies. When planning for cooperative learning, you can use the following guide to ensure you are incorporating each element and choosing an SEL focus area.

Element of Cooperative Learning	Possible SEL Connections (Choose an SEL Focus Area)
Positive Interdependence Are there clear roles and responsibilities? What is the system for accountability?	Relationship Skills (communication, social engagement)

Element of Cooperative Learning	Possible SEL Connections (Choose an SEL Focus Area)
Individual Accountability Is there an individual public performance?	Self-Awareness (recognizing strengths, self-confidence, self-efficacy) Self-Management (goal setting, organizational skills, self-discipline, self-motivation)
Promoting Success of Others How will you incorporate opportunities for appreciations and student demonstration that "my success is your success and your success is my success?"	Relationship Skills (relationship building, teamwork) Social Awareness (appreciating diversity, respect for others)
Interpersonal and Social Skills How will you model and explicitly teach social awareness and relationship skills?	Social Awareness (perspective taking, empathy, appreciating diversity, respect for others) Relationship Skills (communication, social engagement, relationship building, teamwork)
Group Processing What structures have been set up for the group to monitor and reflect on their progress?	Responsible Decision-Making (analyzing situations, solving problems, evaluating, reflecting, ethical responsibility)

Suggestions for Making SEL Explicit

First have students respond to the following prompt individually through writing and then share in small groups before engaging the whole class:

Describe characteristics and observable evidence of collaboration. Make connections to the five SEL competencies. Then invite students to discuss this topic: *What evidence can we look for to demonstrate that our team is collaborating effectively? Make connections to the five SEL competencies.*

From this evidence, coconstruct a collaboration rubric using the language from the SEL competencies that will be used for teams to assess themselves. During the lesson, have groups stop to reflect and self-assess their collaboration and ways they can improve.

SEL SKILLS NEEDED FOR COOPERATIVE LEARNING: QUESTIONS FOR STUDENTS

Name: _____

Learning target: _____

My role and responsibilities: _____

What are the SEL skills I need, and how will I practice and assess these skills in my group?

_____

_____

SEL reflection: How did I do and what do I want to focus on next time?

_____

_____

Expandable PDF (with extra writing space) available for download and printing at http://wwnorton.com/rd/srinivasan

Since there are so many SEL skills integral to cooperative learning, you can also choose one skill to focus on each time you have students engage in cooperative learning. The SEL reflection for cooperative learning on page 95 could also be a useful tool.

Self-Reflection and Self-Assessment

In John Hattie's review of 900 studies of visible learning, one of the highest indicators of a positive impact on student learning was self-reflection (Hattie, 2008). This doesn't mean just having students predict their grades at the end of the term or providing an answer key and having students see how they did but rather continuously providing opportunities for students to be involved in predicting how they will do. This requires teachers to make learning targets and criteria for success clear and ensure they are understood. This teaching practice emphasizes goal setting and monitoring progress toward that goal.

How Self-Reflection Promotes SEL

Self-reflection strengthens intrapersonal SEL competencies. Self-reflection provides an opportunity for students to engage in accurate self-perception, recognizing strengths, fostering self-confidence, and building self-efficacy, which are all facets of self-awareness. Self-reflection can also create a space for growing self-motivation, setting goals, and deepening organizational skills.

Suggestions for Making SEL Explicit

In addition to incorporating self-assessment into every major assignment, when I was in the classroom I had my students set individual academic and SEL goals each week and make plans for how they would achieve their goals. At the end of the week, students reflected on how they did and what they could do to improve their plans for meeting their goal in the following week. I also engaged in one-on-one goal-setting conferences with each student every month. I know this is tough to do given the large number of student contacts secondary teachers have, but it is possible to schedule a five-minute conference with each student monthly if you plan carefully.

Student Voice and Choice

Learning is a social act, and incorporating student voice and choice is vital to creating authentic engagement in secondary classrooms. Students feel that classroom tasks are more important when they are given choices (Marzano, 2011). Choice bolsters intrinsic motivation, effort, and, as a result, learning. To see these benefits, we need to make sure to "create choices that are robust enough for students to feel that their decision has an impact on their learning" (Marzano, 2011). Marzano explains that choice can be provided in four ways: choice of task, choice of reporting formats, choice of learning goals, and choice of behaviors. Student choice empowers students to take ownership of their learning, and in many ways incorporating student choice creates opportunities for students to develop and deepen their voice.

Student voice refers to the "values, opinions, beliefs, perspectives, and cultural backgrounds of individual students and groups of students in a school, and to instructional approaches and techniques that are based on student choices, interests, passions, and ambitions" (Great Schools Partnership, 2013).

When student voice and choice are authentic and not just symbolic it also develops student agency, which is defined as "learning through activities that are meaningful and relevant to learners, driven by their interests, and often self-initiated with appropriate guidance from teachers" (EdWords, n.d.).

GOING DEEPER

In order for students to establish a real sense of agency, it's helpful to spend time developing the Four Learning Mind-Sets (Farrington et al., 2012).

Mind-set #1: A Growth Mind-set. "I can change my intelligence and abilities through effort." First identified and studied by Stanford professor Carol Dweck. Students with a growth mind-set understand that effort is what makes people intelligent, and by focusing on continuous growth they can persist in the face of setbacks. Conversely, when students see intelligence as fixed, they shy away from challenge and give up when things get difficult (Mueller & Dweck, 1998).

Mind-set #2: Self-Efficacy. "I can succeed." Related to the growth mind-set is the belief that one can succeed (Bandura, 1986). Students must believe that they can achieve their goals, and if they need support they will look for alternate ways to develop strategies for success.

Mind-set #3: Sense of Belonging. "I belong in this learning community." When students feel they belong to a learning community and are cared for, they become engaged in learning (Harvey & Schroder, 1963; Oyserman, Bybee, & Terry, 2006).

Mind-set #4: Relevance. "This work has value and purpose for me." Students engage in learning much more enthusiastically and deeply when they value the knowledge and skills that they're working to develop or are interested in.

(Farrington et al., 2012)

How Student Voice and Choice Promotes SEL

Student voice and choice promote SEL development in a number of ways.

Student Choice	Responsible Decision-Making (identifying problems, analyzing situations, solving problems, evaluating, reflecting)
	Self-Awareness (recognizing strengths, self-confidence, self-efficacy)
	Self-Management (self-motivation, goal setting, organizational skills)

Student Voice	Self-Awareness (accurate self-perception, recognizing strengths, self-confidence, self-efficacy)
	Social Awareness (perspective taking, respect for others)
	Relationship Skills (communication, social engagement)

Suggestions for Making SEL Explicit

When creating opportunities for student choice and voice, have students focus on the SEL skills they seek to deepen. Helping students name the specific skill as they engage in it builds their muscles in that particular skill.

Project-Based Learning

At its core, project-based learning (PBL) involves identifying a real-world problem and developing a solution. Students demonstrate what they learn throughout the unit across disciplines rather than just at the end, and the problems they seek to solve usually have them engage with their broader community. Teacher Amber Graeber shared that the goal of PBL is to "give students authentic roles and engage them in solving relevant problems, creating a link between the classroom and our larger community and world." With this technique, classrooms were transformed from "posters and presentations to problem-based experiences" (Graeber, 2012).

At High Tech High in San Diego, students engaged in PBL through testing water quality—when then-governor Arnold Schwarzenegger cut the budget for water quality testing—and educating their community about how they could improve water quality. This interdisciplinary project had students harness their media skills through their humanities classes and analyze scientific data in biology.

How Project-Based Learning Promotes SEL

In *The Employment Mismatch*, employers stated that their employees graduated from four-year colleges without the most critical skills needed for success in the workplace—"adaptability, communication skills, and the ability to solve complex problems" (Fischer, 2013). PBL teaches the skills employers seek.

In *Learning by Heart: The Power of Social-Emotional Learning in Secondary Schools*, project-based learning was identified as a key strategy for creating a curriculum of connection and engagement (Cervonne & Cushman, 2014). After all, SEL is baked into the PBL approach.

Elements of PBL	SEL Connections
Collaboration	Relationship Skills (communication, social engagement, relationship building, teamwork)
	Social Awareness (perspective taking, empathy, appreciating diversity, respect for others)
Manage projects and meet deadlines	Self-Management (self-motivation, goal setting, organizational skills)

Communication and group process skills such as listening and conflict resolution	Relationship Skills (communication, social engagement, relationship building, teamwork)
	Social Awareness (perspective taking, empathy, appreciating diversity, respect for others)
Goal setting	Self-Management (self-motivation, goal setting, organizational skills)
Problem solving	Responsible Decision-Making (identifying problems, analyzing situations, solving problems, evaluating, reflecting, ethical responsibility)
Student voice and choice	Self-Awareness (accurate self-perception, recognizing strengths, self-confidence, self-efficacy)

Suggestions for Making SEL Explicit

Several of the rubrics used for assessment in PBL are Common Core aligned, which also means SEL is embedded. Highlighting the SEL skills used in each rubric and how you plan to teach those skills is a great way to ensure students will have the SEL necessary to succeed with PBL.

GOING DEEPER

Youth-led Participatory Action Research (YPAR) is a powerful SEL approach grounded in social justice where young people are trained to conduct systematic research in order to improve their communities. Learn more at: http://yparhub.berkeley.edu/

Towards an Equitable Classroom

All of these SEL teaching practices and approaches provide a great opportunity to create a more equitable classroom. In a 2018 EdWeek Article, educator, Josh Parker described the 4 C's of an equitable classroom.

1. Counter-Narrative: Teachers must deepen their social awareness SEL competency which can support their understanding of the "negative narratives that persist around the intelligence, beauty and efficacy of our boys and girls of color . . . in the absence of a counter-narrative, promoted by a caring teacher, every damaging narrative has indelible staying power" (Parker, 2018). Having educators engage with and understand the 4 I's of oppression (ideological, institutional, interpersonal and internalized) can be an important starting point when creating the conditions for an equitable classroom.

2. Content (Expertise): Scaffolding and enrichment are central to the teacher's practice as they work to ensure that for every student content is internalized.

3. Control (Continuum): Growth and external control can be at odds and "the quality of equity in any class with traditionally under-

served students can be understood by looking at the imaginary line between control and growth. If the majority of the learning experience is spent on the control side, you can expect growth to be compromised (Parker, 2018)." In an equitable, relationship-centered classroom collaboration not control needs to be the foundation. Incorporating the practices highlighted in Chapter 2 of this book can help create the conditions for a collaborative classroom.

4. Communication (Quality): Creating a classroom where meaning is co-created and not dominated by teacher talk prioritizes authentic student voice and discussion.

GOING DEEPER

Here are some great resources to help incorporate counter-narratives into your classroom practice.

1. *Countering the Narrative* by Jason D. DeHart (Teaching Tolerance, 2017)
2. *Counter-Narrative Curriculum* (The Goalbook Toolkit)

SEL and Common Core

The Common Core State Standards hold the perspective that learning is a social process which calls for teaching practices that take advantage of the power of group work and collaborative learning. Clearly, SEL skills are needed in order to meet the Common Core standards, and even if you may not be implementing the Common Core in your classroom, it may be helpful to see how SEL is integral to these standards so you can get a better sense of how SEL is connected to academic learning. The tables below detail some of the Common Core standards and their connection to SEL competencies. As you review the tables, you will see how the SEL competencies are interdependent. For example, you can't have relationship skills if you aren't socially aware, and you need to be self-aware in order to be socially aware, and so on.

Standard for Mathematical Practice	SEL Connections
Make sense of problems and persevere in solving them.	Students must practice self-awareness to gauge what they know and tap into their strengths. There are also several opportunities to practice self-management as they monitor their progress with solving the problem and work with potentially challenging emotions or self-doubt as they persevere in solving the problem. Students practice social awareness as they reflect on how their classmates may have taken a different approach to solving the problem.
Reason abstractly and quantitatively.	Reasoning requires students to practice self-management through thinking about their thinking.

Standard for Mathematical Practice	SEL Connections
Construct viable arguments and critique the reasoning of others.	Students practice social awareness through understanding the perspectives of others and anticipating how their argument may be received. Relationship skills are practiced as students actively listen to their classmates' arguments. Students engage in self-management as they reflect on their own thinking.
Model with mathematics.	Students practice self-awareness to know what they know in order to make assumptions and approximation and self-manage as they evaluate how their model works.
Use appropriate tools strategically.	Students practice self-management as they determine which tool to use, why, and how use of the tool(s) can deepen their understanding.
Attend to precision.	Students practice social awareness and relationship skills in order to communicate their thought process with precision.
Look for and make use of structure.	Students practice self-awareness as they confidently discern a pattern or structure. They self-manage in order to persist if they cannot find a pattern immediately and monitor their own progress.

Standard for Mathematical Practice	SEL Connections
Look for and express regularity in repeated reasoning.	Students practice self-awareness and self-management as they reflect on and evaluate their work.

English Language Arts Standard	SEL Connections
Describe characters in a story (e.g., their traits, motivations, or feelings) and explain how their actions contribute to the sequence of events.	Students practice social awareness through labeling and recognizing how the characters feel and how their feelings can affect others. Responsible decision making is exercised through reflecting on how character decisions affect situations.
Use technology, including the internet, to produce and publish writing and link to and cite sources as well as to interact and collaborate with others, including linking to and citing sources.	Relationship skills are practiced through collaborating with classmates.
Initiate and participate effectively in a range of collaborative discussions (one-on-one, in groups, and teacher-led) with diverse partners on grade-level topics, texts, and issues, building on others' ideas and expressing their own clearly and persuasively.	Social awareness and relationship skills are built through engaging in a range of academic conversations.

English Language Arts Standard	SEL Connections
Integrate multiple sources of information presented in diverse media or formats (e.g., visually, quantitatively, orally), evaluating the credibility and accuracy of each source.	The responsible decision-making skills of evaluating and reflecting are practiced through utilizing media effectively.
Evaluate a speaker's point of view, reasoning, and use of evidence and rhetoric, identifying any fallacious reasoning or exaggerated or distorted evidence.	Relationship skills, social awareness, and responsible decision making are needed in order to respectfully evaluate another's reasoning and use of evidence.
Present information, findings, and supporting evidence clearly, concisely, and logically such that listeners can follow the line of reasoning, and the organization, development, substance, and style are appropriate to purpose, audience, and task.	Communication skills are critical to presenting effectively.
Make strategic use of digital media (e.g., textual, graphic, audio, visual, and interactive elements) in presentations to enhance understanding of findings, reasoning, and evidence and to add interest.	Responsible decision making is key in order to evaluate the digital media used in presentations.

English Language Arts Standard	SEL Connections
Adapt speech to a variety of contexts and tasks, demonstrating command of formal English when indicated or appropriate.	Social awareness is essential to being able to adapt speech to various situations.

Now that the connections between SEL and some Common Core standards have been made explicit, here are some examples of how you can attend to the SEL skills needed in order to meet the standard.

Helping Students Meet the Standards with SEL Skills

Math

STANDARD

Make sense of problems and persevere in solving them.

SEL COMPETENCIES NEEDED

Self-awareness

Self-management

Social awareness

TEACHING TIPS

- After having students restate the problem in their own words to check for understanding, have them exercise their self-awareness muscle and identify what skills (e.g., concentration) and understanding (e.g., use of formulas) are needed to solve the problem.
- Recognize and normalize any stressful feelings in the room.
- Help students tap into their confidence by having them reflect on when they've successfully solved a similar problem.
- When students get stuck, have them reconnect with what they already know about the problem and how to solve it.

STANDARD

Construct viable arguments and critique the reasoning of others.

SEL COMPETENCIES NEEDED

Self-management
Social awareness
Relationship skills

TEACHING TIPS

- Instead of having students explain their thinking, have students explain their partners' thinking to promote active listening.
- Model how to ask good follow-up questions with a sample problem and student volunteer.

- Have students utilize sentence stems that require them to restate their classmates' viewpoints before stating their own. For example, _____ [student's name]'s approach to solving the problem utilized _____ and while I got the same answer, I had a different approach using the following steps: _____.
- Remind students to practice class norms and agreements and let classmates explain their thinking without interruption.

English Language Arts

STANDARD

Initiate and participate effectively in a range of collaborative discussions (one-on-one, in groups, and teacher-led) with diverse partners on grade-level topics, texts, and issues, building on others' ideas and expressing their own clearly and persuasively.

SEL COMPETENCIES NEEDED

Self-management
Social awareness
Relationship skills

TEACHING TIPS

- Once SEL is established in your classroom, through, for example, a lesson like the one offered in Chapter 2 around making SEL competencies explicit in circle practice, you can have students identify the

SEL skills they need at the start of each lesson when you share the learning target and then invite students to share how the class can explicitly practice that skill and assess it.

- Utilizing the lesson offered in Chapter 2 on coconstructing agreements can also provide an important foundation for respectful classroom discussions.

SEL and Next-Generation Science Standards

Like the Common Core State Standards, the Next Generation Science Standards seek to streamline what students should be learning in each grade and prepare them for college and career. Curricula that meet the science standards are infused with SEL through cooperative learning tasks, self-assessment, and the use of the claim, evidence, reasoning framework for scientific discussion.

SEL and Personalized Learning

Personalized learning involves "tailoring learning for each student's strengths, needs and interests—including enabling student voice and choice in what, how, when and where they learn—to provide flexibility and supports to ensure mastery of the highest standards possible" (Abel, 2016). Personalized learning presents many opportunities for SEL development, especially in intrapersonal skills. For example, most personalized learning has individual learner profiles that outline strengths and areas of growth (self-awareness), and there is daily attention to goal setting and progress monitoring (self-management). Students are also given more choice, which requires many aspects of responsible decision making. After all, self-directed learning is an SEL skill!

SEL and College and Career Pathways

Linked Learning is a successful high school improvement strategy grounded in rigor, relevance, and relationships, where education is delivered in industry-specific themes as teachers collaborate across disciplines and incorporate input from professionals within the industry, and students also engage in work-based learning. During my time in Oakland, I've had the opportunity to partner with our Linked Learning office in a number of ways through offering SEL-targeted professional learning. One particularly effective professional learning experience helped teachers see how integral SEL is to success in the workplace. I had teachers reflect on the SEL skills they themselves needed in order to get and keep a job, and after that they cross-walked the five core SEL competencies with the attributes employers want.

ATTRIBUTES EMPLOYERS SEEK
IN ORDER OF IMPORTANCE

Problem-solving skills

Ability to work in a team

Communication skills (written)

Leadership

Communication skills (verbal)

Strong work ethic

Analytical skills/quantitative skills

Communication skills (verbal)

Initiative

Detail-oriented

Flexibility/adaptability

Technical skills

Interpersonal skills

Computer skills

Organizational ability

Strategic planning skills

Creativity

Friendly/outgoing personality

Tactfulness

Entrepreneurial skills/risk taking

(2018 Job Outlook Survey, National Association of Colleges and Employers)

From these two engagements, it became clear to them that they had to prioritize the teaching of SEL skills. In partnership with our career technical education specialists, I offered the following activity using real scenarios experienced by our students:

WORK-BASED LEARNING IN LINKED LEARNING:
MAKING SEL CONNECTIONS

We offer a few scenarios as exemplars for what can occur in work-based learning situations when students clash with the dominant culture. Scan all scenarios and then choose one that piques your interest. On your own, consider the scenario and then predict some of the emotions students might experience and how that might impact their learning and their participation. Which SEL skills could a student draw upon to navigate this situation? Jot your ideas down on the chart, or wherever you like.

Form a group with a few other folks who chose the same scenario, and share your jottings with each other. Together, quick draft a mini lesson to teach the SEL skills identified to support student success in this context. When planning a mini lesson, consider the subtle moments that cause students anxiety, and proactively teach the skills and habits that would support students to persist. We will be sharing highlights from our mini lesson and reflections with the larger group.

In the context of our mini lesson, how can we plan ahead to:
- Teach students to be aware of their emotions and the emotions of others
- Teach students a menu of skills and habits that might help them manage these situations

(continued)

- Provide students opportunities to practice these skills and habits
- Provide students opportunities to reflect on how well they handled a situation and brainstorm what they might do differently next time

For each scenario given, answer the following four questions:

- How might the student feel in this situation?
- What might be happening to the student's participation and learning?
- Which SEL skills would help the student navigate this situation?
- What might be a good contextualized mini lesson to teach students the SEL skills to handle this type of situation?

Scenarios

1. Jonathan has 15 minutes to get to work. It's a 25-minute bus ride and the bus is running late. Jonathan remembers the last time he was late, and his boss said it was no big deal.

2. Tahiri's supervisor requested that she set up a spreadsheet for the data she was collecting for the office. Tahiri worked on the spreadsheet for two days, making sure it was just right. She was very excited to show her supervisor the work. At the weekly meeting, her coworker, Ms. Delina, said she created the spreadsheet instead. Tahiri's supervisor said they would use Ms. Delina's spreadsheet.

3. Markus came into the office on the first day of his internship. He wore his

best jeans and tied his dreads back. He was surprised to see that everyone in the office appeared to be in their 60s, male, and white. One of his supervisor's first comments to him was, "Around here, we wear belts and shoes without designs on the outside."

4. Tara is in the middle of collating and stapling a large number of documents for a presentation her supervisor, Joelle, is making the next day. Joelle comes in and asks Tara to make a few phone calls to clients who will be at the presentation. An hour later, Joelle asks if the calls have been made. Tara is confused—she has continued to do the collating and stapling job, not clear that the calls should have been prioritized.

Final Reflections

What came up for you when you engaged with these scenarios? How similar or different are your students' experiences with work-based learning?

What will you take away from today's engagement?

Note From the Field

Instructional rounds is a process for school improvement inspired by medical rounds that's grounded in inquiry and focuses on "understanding what's happening in classrooms, how we as a system produce those effects, and how we can move closer to producing the learning we want to see" (City, 2011). During the 2014–2015 school year, I served as an instructional rounds facilitator, and every school in our district identified a problem of practice around how students engage in academic discussion and an SEL focus. Educators from across the system (teachers, principals, curriculum experts, and principal supervisors) then visited classrooms to gather evidence around patterns of students' learning inclusive of SEL. This was a great way to have every leader understand the interconnectedness of student mastery of content goals and SEL and create goals based on data that were academic, social, and emotional.

What are some ways SEL can be part of ongoing improvement efforts at your school?

Are there already structures for gathering observable evidence on SEL within an academic context at your school?

Starting Where You Are

In this chapter, you were introduced to a few key SEL teaching practices that can be used across content and grade level, and explored the relationship between SEL and Common Core, personalized learning, and aspects of college and career readiness.

You are probably already engaging in the SEL teaching practices highlighted in this chapter. Choose one practice that makes SEL more intentional. If this is a practice your whole teaching team engages in often, maybe you can work together to make SEL more explicit in your instruction.

SEL in Lesson Planning: Tools and Resources

The alternative to good design is always bad design. There's no such thing as no design.
—Adam Judge, designer

Teachers are at their core designers, and we design one of the most important things in the world—learning experiences. In my work as a teacher, educational leader, and professional developer, the number one factor influencing success is undoubtedly the time and care I put into designing the unit, lesson, meeting agenda, or professional learning experience. Unless you plan with SEL in mind, it's unlikely your lesson will have SEL integrated into it explicitly. This chapter provides tools and resources around how you can incorporate SEL into your lesson design and integrate SEL into your lesson planning process.

HIGH SCHOOL HUMANITIES TEACHER
AND TEACHER COACH

I believe that social and emotional learning is the fabric of being a person, and academic learning depends on it. As I work to figure out how to place students at the center of my teaching, I've found small choices matter, like greeting each student by name and learning how to pronounce their names correctly, having a ritualized way to celebrate birthdays, or playing a student-selected song during each transition between classes. These choices can add up to a feeling of connectedness that makes it more likely for students to take the social risks involved in learning and to support each other along the way. During lesson planning, I work to ask myself, "Why might this matter to students?" "Does this lesson rely on me telling them that, or can they discover it?" and "Is there room yet for students to bring their own connections to this?" I've often seen the answers to those questions shape students' engagement and self-efficacy in the course. And when I've been able to tend to my own social and emotional well-being, my teaching has grown so much more because I'm more able to take in the feedback students have invested back into the class. Their feedback comes in a lot of forms. For example, I facilitate a unit focused on research skills in which each student crafts and investigates their own historical question. A few years ago I started the habit of developing a new unit each summer based on a question that multiple students had independently chosen. Most recently, I built a thematic unit about the relationship between Haiti and the Dominican Republic over time. And it's been one of the most incredible units to teach because it was born out of cultural and linguistic knowledge students introduced me to and a question they had deep curiosity about—they cultivated my social awareness, an SEL skill I value. In that unit, students read a fictional anchor text alongside primary historical sources so that they can analyze the extent to which the core text tells the full story. It is really a living unit because each time I've taught it, student analysis about the impact of missing perspectives in the anchor text, or their thoughts about the ways in which people's emotional lives can motivate their actions and thus shape history, grows in nuance and informs how I teach it the next time round.

Molly McKay Bryson, Dearborn STEM Academy,
Boston Public Schools, Roxbury, Massachusetts

The Teacher's SEL Practice

In Chapter 3 we explored key SEL teaching practices that promote SEL in our students. What we didn't discuss was how critical a teacher's own SEL practice is to teaching SEL. In fact, research confirms that teachers who were mandated to teach SEL but didn't cultivate their own SEL practice actually worsened their students' SEL skills (Hagelskamp, Brackett, Rivers, & Salovey, 2013), while teachers who developed SEL skills not only improved their own well-being but improved the academic learning and social-emotional development of their students (Flook et al., 2013). In the SEL integrated instruction lesson plan offered in this chapter, you will see that each lesson not only requires you to reflect on the student SEL focus but also asks you to choose an SEL focus for yourself.

Teaching is incredibly complex: on average, teachers make 1,500 educational decisions every school day (M, 2016). Having a strong SEL practice can help us make better decisions in service of our students because we are less reactive and understand them better. One of the ways in which we can begin to grow and deepen our own SEL practice is to reflect on our own SEL as we design our lessons. Here are some suggested guiding questions:

1. What beliefs do I have about my students that may be impacting my instruction or lesson design? How do these beliefs help or hinder my students and myself? (self-awareness)
2. How can this lesson affirm the identities of the students in my class? (social awareness)
3. How am I placing myself in my students' shoes as I design this lesson? (social awareness)
4. How is this lesson relevant to the lives of my students? (social awareness)
5. How will I model SEL in this lesson? (Get specific, for example:

"I will practice mindfulness with my students so I can be more fully present." "I will share how I utilized a growth mind-set in my work." (self-awareness)

6. How will I strengthen my relationship skills with my students through this lesson? What specific actions can I take? (relationship skills)

7. How will I practice self-management and name how I'm practicing it during this lesson? (self-management)

Begin With the End in Mind

One of my favorite habits in *The Seven Habits of Highly Successful People* is to "begin with the end in mind" (Covey, 1989). What this essentially means is that we are clear about the outcome or goal we wish to achieve, and from that goal we make a plan. Similarly, one of the most popular ways of designing curriculum and learning experiences is backward design. Backward design involves setting learning goals and then choosing the instructional practices and ways of assessing to reach that goal. The backward design process has three main elements: (1) identifying the results sought, (2) determining the evidence that will show the results were achieved, and (3) designing the learning activities that will achieve the desired results (Wiggins & McTighe, 2008). Each of these elements asks key questions:

1. Identifying the learning goal asks: what should students know,

understand, and be able to do? I would add an additional aspect to this important planning question and also ask, how should students feel? In our SEL professional development planning in Oakland, our former SEL coordinator, who now works as a CASEL professional development consultant, Mary Hurley, encouraged us to reflect on how we'd want participants to feel. Even though we can't guarantee they would feel a certain way, just like we can't guarantee all students will always learn exactly what we set out to have them learn, we can create the conditions for supporting all our learners and also be intentional about our facilitation and design of the learning experience to increase the likelihood that participants and students would feel a certain way. This question should also take into account both academic and SEL goals.

2. Determining the evidence asks: what will I accept as evidence that student understanding occurred? Evidence of SEL can be collected through teacher observation, self-assessment, performance assessment, or a combination of two or all three. For example, self-assessment can be used to reflect on one's SEL skills, as in the reflection forms offered in Chapter 3. Teacher observation could involve you circling around the room and having an observation checklist where you take note of how each student may be displaying behaviors that indicate SEL competencies, like not interrupting when their classmates are speaking (self-management). Performance assessments, also known as authentic assessments, are more

complex, and they are process or product oriented. For example, in a ninth grade biology unit on stress and the brain, students play the role of a physiologist hired by the school district to evaluate stress management claims being proposed for a health campaign for youth in the community. SEL can clearly be integrated through this unit in a number of ways, but incorporating ways to assess SEL in each lesson does not take the place of a comprehensive, well-established, valid, and reliable SEL assessment (AIR, 2016) that can really gauge where students are with specific SEL skills.

3. Design a learning plan that will achieve the desired results asks: what knowledge and skills (inclusive of SEL) will students need to achieve the desired results? This is where we decide which SEL teaching practices we need to employ and what resources we will use.

SEL Learning Targets: Shifting From I to We

The first thing students need to learn is what they're supposed to be learning. If you own a global positioning system (GPS), you probably can't imagine taking a trip without it. Unlike a printed map, a GPS provides up-to-the-minute information about where you are, the distance to your destination, how long until you get there, and exactly what to do when you make a wrong turn. But a GPS can't do any of that without a precise description of where you want to go. Think of shared learning targets in the same way. They

> convey to students the destination for the lesson—what to learn, how deeply to learn it, and exactly how to demonstrate their new learning. (Moss, Brookhart, & Long, 2011)

Early on in my teaching practice, I worked with an instructional coach who helped me see how crucial it was to have shared learning targets in student-friendly language using "I can" statements so students were clear on exactly what they should be able to know and do by the end of the lesson. What took my teaching to the next level was coconstructing the learning targets with my students. This was a great way to incorporate student voice and also make sure my students were clear on what we were learning as they generated success criteria for the learning targets. Finally, instead of using "I" in our learning targets, I shifted the language to "we," which gave a sense of how as a class we would support each other in our learning and be responsible for each other's success. This sentiment reinforced community building and collectivism in the class. Particularly when we think about SEL learning targets, there's power in using "we" instead of "I."

When our school district partnered with EL Education to implement their ELA curriculum in our middle schools, I saw an opportunity to make SEL explicit in the curriculum, given their emphasis on learning targets. I went through all of the protocols used to support instruction, which was where the DNA of SEL lived in their curriculum, and developed SEL learning targets using "we" language for each protocol.

Below are SEL learning target examples you can draw from for each competency:

SELF-AWARENESS

- We can identify what we understand and learned (from today's lesson) and what we still need more support with.
- We can identify when we need help and who can provide it.
- We can self-assess and reflect on our own progress.
- We can identify our strengths and our areas for growth.
- We can share our background knowledge of the topic we are exploring
- We can identify what we already know and what we would like to learn.
- We can practice our reflection skills.
- We can notice our feelings and thoughts as we engage in the protocol (e.g., concentric circles).
- We can prepare ourselves for the protocol (e.g., discussion appointments) by being aware of our feelings and thoughts about participating.
- We can share our thinking with confidence.
- We can demonstrate awareness of our personal rights and responsibilities during the protocol (e.g., fishbowl).
- We can reflect on the important ideas in our current learning.
- We can use prior knowledge along with new knowledge to make meaning.
- We can demonstrate awareness of our personal responsibilities during the protocol (e.g., jigsaw).
- We can identify our strengths and our areas for growth.
- We can check for understanding and identify what we may still need more support with.

- We can identify when we do not understand a word in our reading, look up the definition, and write it in our notebooks in our own words.
- We can use anchor charts to self-assess and reflect on our own progress.
- We can annotate text to show our thinking and feelings about what we're reading.

SELF-MANAGEMENT

- We can manage ourselves in order to participate productively in the protocol (e.g., back to back and face to face or concentric circles).
- We can describe and demonstrate ways to express emotions in a socially acceptable manner.
- We can be mindful of our air time so everyone has a chance to share in our group.
- We can offer and receive constructive feedback in order to grow as writers.
- We can reflect on the text prior to academic discussion in order to participate fully.
- We can stay focused on the topic of discussion.
- We can manage and express emotions, thoughts, impulses, and stress in constructive ways.
- We can learn from our mistakes.
- We can set, track, and evaluate our progress toward goals.
- We can annotate text in order to support our goals around understanding what we're reading.

SOCIAL AWARENESS

- We can have empathy for other people's emotions, perspectives, cultures, languages, and histories.
- We can identify the feelings and understand the intentions of others.
- We can participate productively in the protocol (e.g., turn to your partner)
- We can support our group to make sure everyone gets the chance to speak.
- We contribute productively to our group.
- We can practice the protocol (e.g., chalk talk) effectively to make sure all voices are heard.
- We can make sure partners balance air time during the protocol (e.g., discussion appointments).
- We can practice the norms of being kind, specific, and helpful along with I statements and warm and cool feedback in order to support the learning and growth of our classmates.
- We can respect other students through exhibiting open-mindedness and valuing others' contributions.
- We can practice active listening through building on one another's ideas by referring to them.
- We can use specific examples from the text to explain our points.
- We can give input and ensure participation.
- We can ask clarifying and probing questions that push the conversation further and deeper when appropriate.
- We can participate in collaborative annotation to practice contributing productively to our classroom community.

RELATIONSHIP SKILLS

- We can practice active listening in order to learn from our classroom community.
- We can respect diverse perspectives.
- We can communicate clearly and effectively.
- We can be welcoming and respectful to everyone as we participate in the protocol (e.g., chalk talk)
- We can practice the protocol (e.g., world cafe) effectively to make sure all voices are heard and everyone contributes equitably.
- We can share our ideas respectfully.
- We can work effectively in our pairs.
- We can listen to others' ideas, questions, and opinions with openness and respect.

RESPONSIBLE DECISION-MAKING

- We can consider the well-being of self and others when making decisions.
- We can adapt our speech and behavior to the purpose of the protocol and in support of the community of learners.
- We can practice the norms our class coconstructed in order to support the learning and growth of our classmates.
- We can behave responsibly when engaged in annotating text.

Students then crafted success criteria for the SEL learning target and evidence. The most common way to support students in brainstorming success criteria was to use a T chart and have them detail collectively what the learning target looks like and sounds like. These T charts were saved and posted in the classroom so whenever we had a similar SEL learning target again, we could refer to it.

Unit or Lesson Planning Guide With SEL Integrated

What follows is a modified guide and template rooted in backward design that incorporates SEL and can be used for both unit and lesson planning. For those of you unfamiliar with lesson planning using an understanding by design approach, here are some clarifications so you can best utilize this guide.

Essential questions and enduring understandings are critical when designing units of study. Essential questions as defined by Wiggins and McTighe, the creators of Understanding by Design, are "questions that are not answerable with finality in a brief sentence. . . . Their aim is to stimulate thought, to provoke inquiry, and to spark more questions—including thoughtful student questions—not just pat answers" (Wiggins & McTighe, 2008). Enduring understandings synthesize what we want students to take away from the learning that has value beyond a particular unit of study and can even transfer to adult life. For example, when I crafted a unit on mindfulness tied to National Health Education Standards for my middle schoolers, the enduring understanding was that mindfulness can help us manage our lives more effectively, and the essential questions we explored throughout the unit were: (1) What is mindfulness? (2) How can I be mindful? (3) Why should I be mindful?

There is a difference between overarching essential questions that help frame the many subtopics within a larger topic or unit and topic-specific essential questions that cover only a specific topic. For example, in our district's ninth grade biology unit on stress, the enduring understanding is that acute stress is an evolutionary adaptation; however, chronic stress can cause damage to physiological and neurological processes. The overarching essential question is, Is stress good or bad? Topic-specific essential questions or supporting questions include these: Does the body respond to all stressful stimuli in the same way? How is the stress response an adaptation? What are the potential negative consequences of the stress response?

The following are some examples of SEL essential questions and enduring understandings from a unit that has students work as a team of aeronautical engineers investigating designs for aeronautical devices to develop a prototype and model showing a slow landing device.

Enduring understanding: It's okay to not have the answers or get something right the first time. The process of learning from mistakes is more important.

Essential questions: How did your team go about completing the task? What was your process? How did you team end up with this design? How did your group work together successfully? What did each person do? What challenged your group? How could your group have collaborated more successfully?

SEL INTERGRATED LESSON PLAN TEMPLATE

PART 1

Desired Results: What should students know, understand, and be able to do, and how will they feel as a result of the lesson?

Goals/Standards (academic and SEL goals are explicit and interdependent):

_____

_____

Teacher SEL Focus (choose one):

Suggested guiding questions:

- What beliefs do I have about my students that may be impacting my instruction or lesson design? How do these beliefs help or hinder my students and myself? (self-awareness)
- How can this lesson affirm the identities of the students in my class? (social awareness)
- How am I incorporating a counter-narrative? (social awareness)
- How am I placing myself in my students' shoes as I design this lesson? (social awareness)
- How is this lesson relevant to the lives of my students? (social awareness)
- How will I model SEL in this lesson? Get specific, for example: "I will practice mindfulness with my students so I can be more fully present." "I will share how I utilized a growth mind-set in my work." (self-awareness)
- How will I strengthen my relationship skills with my students through this lesson? What specific actions can I take? (relationship skills)
- How will I practice self-management and name how I'm practicing it during this lesson? (self-management)

(continued)

Understandings
(inclusive of SEL):
Students will understand that . . .

Essential questions
(inclusive of SEL):

Students will:

be able to know . . .   be able to do . . .   feel . . .

Learning Targets (inclusive of SEL):

PART 2
Evidence: What will students do to show what they have learned? What are the success criteria?

Detail authentic performance tasks
that will demonstrate student
understanding of desired results
(inclusive of SEL):

Detail the criteria that performances
of understanding will be evaluated
by (inclusive of SEL):

Detail additional evidence (quizzes, homework, etc.) that will show desired results:

Detail the ways in which students will practice reflection and self-assessment (self-awareness SEL competency) on academic and SEL learning targets:

PART 3:

What learning experiences and instruction will lead to the desired results?

When planning a unit, this section should be adapted. Discuss the three signature SEL practices (welcoming rituals, engaging practices, and optimistic closings) and the learning activities more broadly.

In developing Part 3, utilizing Understanding by Design's WHERETO guide can be useful.

"How will the design: W = Help the students know Where the unit is going and What is expected? Help the teacher know Where the students are coming from (prior knowledge, interests)? H = Hook all students and Hold their interest? E = Equip students, help them Experience the key ideas and Explore the issues? R = Provide opportunities to Rethink and Revise their understandings and work? E = Allow students to Evaluate their work and its implications? T = Be Tailored (personalized) to the different needs, interests and abilities of learners? O = Be Organized to maximize initial and sustained engagement as well as effective learning?" (Wiggins & McTighe, 2008).

(continued)

Welcoming Ritual:
Welcoming rituals support contribution by all voices, reinforce norms for respectful listening, allow students to connect, and create a sense of belonging. These are not just team builders, disconnected from the learning of the day. Be sure to detail how this is connected to the learning targets (inclusive of SEL).

SEL Teaching Practices and Engaging Practices:

What SEL teaching practices detailed in Chapter 3 can you use? (academic discussion, cooperative learning, self-reflection and self-assessment, student voice and choice, etc.)

How do you plan to make SEL explicit in your instruction?

How will engaging practices be incorporated in your instruction, and how will SEL be made explicit?
(Engaging practices are infused with SEL, vary in complexity, and consist of sequential steps facilitated by the teacher to support learning individually and collectively, like the use of turn to your partner, world café, or jigsaw.)

How will you ensure student talk exceeds teacher talk? What structures or engaging practices will be set up to support purposeful, equitable, student interaction?

Supporting all learners: Taking into account individualized education programs and differentiation, detail strategies for supporting all learners paying special attention to scaffolding and enrichment.

Brain breaks: When and how will you incorporate brain breaks and opportunities for students to breathe, stretch, and integrate their new learning?

Student Feedback: How are you gathering student feedback on the lesson?

(continued)

Learning Plan

Time	Facilitation Instructions (teaching/ engaging practices, materials, grouping, progress monitoring, etc.):	SEL Connections
Ex. 5 minutes	Welcoming ritual: Once students arrive in pairs, share the following prompt: We are all individuals with unique personalities. How can we work together? After students have come up with lists individually, they discuss their answers with a partner and, depending on class time available, possible answers are discussed and a student charts answers while the teacher facilitates.	Social awareness Relationship skills

Optimistic Closing:

How can you incorporate reflections, appreciations, and positive ways to reinforce learning? Examples include:

Think of . . .
• Something I learned today that I'm excited to learn more about
• Someone I appreciate and why
• Something I enjoyed about class
• An SEL skill I practiced well and an SEL skill I want to get better at
• An appreciation, apology, or aha . . .

PART 4:
Teacher Reflection and Student Feedback

How and what did my students learn? What's my evidence?

How did my students feel? What's my evidence?

What student feedback did I receive, and how do I plan to incorporate it in upcoming lessons?

How did I do with my SEL teacher focus? How do I know?

What changes do I want to make for my next lesson? Why?

Expandable PDF (with extra writing space) available for download and printing at http://wwnorton.com/rd/srinivasan

Note From the Field

The average tenure of an urban superintendent is three and a half years (Council of the Great City Schools, 2010). Given the frequent changes in leadership and the effects those changes can have on district-wide initiatives, staffing, and funding, a key strategy in baking SEL into the system that's hard to undo is to make SEL part of performance frameworks. For example, in Oakland, SEL is an integral part of our homegrown principal and teacher evaluations. Three widely used professional teaching frameworks that support educator growth and development—(1) the Classroom Assessment Scoring System, (2) Danielson's Framework for Teaching, and (3) Marzano's Observational Protocol—all support SEL (Yoder, 2014).

What are some ways your teacher growth and development systems are already supporting SEL?

Just as SEL can be integrated into educator growth and development systems, SEL can be integrated into student performance assessments. For example, in Oakland all seniors complete a graduate capstone project, in which they choose a topic, conduct original field research, write a research paper, and present orally to an audience that includes school and community members. All facets of this performance assessment require SEL, and in order to set students up for success, teachers have been intentionally teaching SEL skills.

How is SEL already part of performance assessments in your context?

Starting Where You Are

Now you are probably realizing how integral and interdependent SEL is with academic learning. Choose one SEL competency to focus on each week or unit. For instance, the Metropolitan Nashville Public School District created an SEL scope and sequence for the entire district, designating a specific SEL competency focus area in every grade level and content area for a duration of nine weeks.

Reflective Practice: How Do I Know If This Is Making a Difference?

Innovation floats on a sea of inquiry and that curiosity is a driver for change. Creating the conditions in schools and learning settings where curiosity is encouraged, developed and sustained is essential to opening up thinking, changing practice and creating dramatically more innovative approaches to learning and teaching.

—Timperley, Halbert, and Kaser (2014)

Reflective practice involves thinking critically and analyzing one's work with the intention of improving one's professional practice. Open questions are a key part of this process. Open questions, questions that require more thought and cannot be answered with a simple yes or no, are the most powerful tools available for our personal and professional growth.

Open questions can literally "hijack the brain" through triggering a mental reflex called "instinctive elaboration" (Hoffeld, 2017). Often when we hear an open question, our minds instantly start to ponder an answer and we can't think of anything else. In fact, decades of research confirm that the more our brain reflects on a certain behavior, the more likely we will engage in it. So even if all you did was just ask yourself, "How can I integrate SEL into my instruction more explicitly?," it's likely your teaching practice will incorporate more SEL.

JUNIOR SCHOOL PRINCIPAL

Reflective practice means pausing to create space and openness to hover above and around practice. As a leader I know that some key conditions for reflective practice involve time, mind-set, and culture. Right now I have a task force composed of six teachers and an assistant principal looking at how we use our time, and they are trying to iterate new schedules that prioritize social-emotional and ethical learning and time for teacher reflection, collaboration, and conversation. Regarding mind-set, reflective practice requires having a predisposition to identify and critically examine our assumptions to renew or realign practice or shift the system toward what we truly value. The SEL competencies of self-awareness and self-management are really important here, because we are asking, "Is what we are doing really serving our students? Where's the evidence?"

Reflective practice is fueled in a climate of trust. There is such a value and need for colleagues to see and experience one another's practice, and in order to feel safe enough to do that you need to build trust, and this takes time. The same way you build community in the classroom, you need to build community with your teachers. We've invested in creating smaller professional learning communities and protocols that share common language and lead to collegial communication. This helps to create a solid, safe platform to look at practice critically and allows colleagues to diverge without discord, which is a key part of assumptions hunting.

Dr. Paris Priore-Kim, Punahou School, Honolulu, Hawaii

Reflective practice is not only a transformative way of using data to improve teaching but also helps educators deepen their own SEL competencies. It is one of the most powerful tools in practice-based professional learning. Through holding an inquiry stance we create the conditions for shifting our practice by making reflection an integral part of our lives. This chapter offers some structured ways for busy educators to build reflection into their teaching practice, including a discussion around cultivating a reflective disposition, SEL-focused teacher inquiry, SEL learning walk tools, and feedback protocols.

In "Building a New Structure for School Leadership," Richard Elmore (1999), director of the Doctor of Educational Leadership (EdLD) program at the Harvard Graduate School of Education, affirms that a hurdle in student achievement is the reality that most teachers work in isolation and don't have the opportunity to engage in collaboration with their colleagues. Many of the resources provided in this chapter promote collaboration among colleagues in service of SEL at both the adult and student levels with the hope of supporting collective teacher efficacy. Collective teacher efficacy is a belief shared by staff that through their collective action, they can positively influence student outcomes. With an effect size of 1.57, collective teacher efficacy is ranked as the number one factor influencing student achievement (Brinson & Steiner, 2007).

Cultivating a Reflective Disposition Strengthens Our Own Adult SEL Competencies

American philosopher, psychologist, and education reformer John Dewey emphasized that reflection has three main elements. The first involves a process or systematic way of thinking and an end product that illustrates one's meaning making. The second element of reflection consists of three mind-sets that cultivate a reflective disposition: open-mindedness, whole-heartedness, and responsibility. The third element maintains that any real reflection has language and communication, which is most likely achieved through conversation with colleagues. What truly distinguishes merely reflecting from being a reflective practitioner, however, is the degree to which we cultivate the qualities of open-mindedness, wholeheartedness, and responsibility. Open-mindedness requires us to strengthen several of our SEL competencies (self-awareness, social awareness, and relationship skills). To cultivate open-mindedness, we need to be willing to look and listen deeply to alternative points of view and consider new ideas. In her widely popular TEDx Talk "The Power of Vulnerability," Brene Brown used the term "wholehearted" to refer to people who fully embraced vulnerability and operated their lives from a place of worthiness. Similarly, in Dewey's work wholeheartedness implies that educators can overcome their fears and uncertainties in an effort to continuously review their practice as they throw themselves fully into their work (Farrell, 2014). Whole-heartedness also requires us to deepen many of our SEL competencies including self-awareness and self-management. Finally, an attitude of responsibility takes into account the impact of our reflections on ourselves, our students, and the community in which we teach (Farrell, 2014), thus strengthening our responsible decision-making SEL competency. Take a moment to think deeply about the following questions:

- What are some ways you are already cultivating a reflective disposition?
- How do the qualities of open-mindedness, wholeheartedness, and responsibility show up in your work?
- What are some ways you may want to strengthen and deepen these qualities?

SEL-Focused Teacher Inquiry

My most powerful professional experiences when I was in the classroom involved teacher research, an academic reflective practice that really looks at the teacher as the central figure of change or transformation. Through this process of intentional, systematic inquiry, my students became my most important teachers.

In an interview with *EdWeek*, Anna Richert, founder of Mills Teacher Scholars, an organization that supports teachers in systematically reflecting on their teaching practice, shared that while "all good teachers reflect on their practice to make sense of their work, those who engage in teacher research do this reflection in a deep and intentional manner" (2011). She identifies three core practices that are part of the teacher research process: (1) to carefully formulate a research question; (2) to conceptualize and enact a systematic and intentional plan for gathering and analyzing classroom and school-based data to answer that question; and (3) to articulate and enact a plan for changed classroom practice that reflects the teacher's learning from the research process. Central to this entire process is taking the time to think individually and collaboratively with colleagues about what's happening in your classroom and placing understanding students at the heart of one's work.

In Oakland, several Mills Teacher Scholars have developed SEL-focused research questions that identified SEL skills that support student learning and explored how they can teach those skills. While many teachers have found the experience of working with organizations like Mills Teacher

Scholars transformational, not every school has the resources to support this type of inquiry-based professional learning. Still, we can incorporate some elements of this approach into our own professional learning plans and collaboration at our school sites.

1. DEVELOP AN SEL INQUIRY FOCUS

Perhaps you and a colleague or your department or grade-level team can develop an SEL inquiry focus. For example, maybe your focus is on one of the SEL teaching practices discussed in Chapter 3 of this book. After you land on a focus, try to create an "If . . . then . . ." statement that links a teaching practice or strategy and student learning. Then, you can adapt it into an "If . . . will . . ." question. For example, "If I teach students active listening, will their ability to participate more effectively in academic discussion improve?"

2. CHOOSE FOCAL STUDENTS

Pick one to three students that you will reflect on more deeply in relation to your SEL inquiry focus. For example, if your SEL inquiry focus is academic discussion, then you will want to pay special attention to their participation in academic discussion.

3. COLLECT DATA

The term "data" is used rather loosely here, to include anything that gives insight into how students are thinking, learning, and feeling. Interviews with students that have them reflect on their learning, student work, or a video recording of students engaging in an academic task are all great data sources. Try to collect data every two weeks or at the very least once a month.

4. REFLECT ON DATA INDIVIDUALLY AND COLLABORATIVELY

Carve out time (ideally every week or two but no less than monthly) to look deeply at your data, first individually and then with colleagues. Think about what success looks like with respect to the SEL skills or academic task you are trying to teach. For example, what does it look like to participate effectively in academic discussion? What does successful active listening look like? You can adapt the mindful consultancy protocol on page 150 to support group reflection.

5. SHIFT YOUR TEACHING BASED ON WHAT YOU LEARN

Based on your reflections, decide on one practical change you can make to your teaching practice. For example, if your individual and collaborative reflection on your data reveals that your students need you to scaffold more, then make a plan for how you will do that and enlist your colleagues in checking in with you on how that goes.

Remember, teacher inquiry is an iterative process, and these five steps are just a guide to get started so you can be more intentional about SEL in your teaching practice. Inquiry is challenging for individual teachers to do in isolation from their colleagues or from leaders, so engage your principal or colleagues in doing this together. Below is a table you can use along with your colleagues to organize your SEL-focused inquiry.

MINDFUL CONSULTANCY

A mindful consultancy is a structured way for helping colleagues think more expansively about a question they are holding in their work. It is adapted from the Consultancy Protocol, which was developed by Gene Thompson and the National School Reform Faculty, Harmony Education Center. By infusing the Consultancy Protocol with mindful breathing and an SEL skill reflection, we are more inclined to be fully present as our colleagues share and offer their best guidance and reflections while also lifting up the SEL skills we practiced and deepened through engaging in this protocol.

Mindful Consultancy Protocol

Estimated Time: 16 minutes per participant. Select a timekeeper and the order of sharing.

1. (30 seconds) Practice mindful breathing with your partner(s). It may be helpful to focus on the following phrases during the breathing periods:

   Breathing in, I listen to my colleagues. Breathing out, I hear what they say.

2. (3 minutes) The presenter gives an overview of the inquiry question, focal students, and data. This is also a time to offer some context and possibly explore the SEL skills needed to be successful in the academic task and what the presenter is noticing around the data.

3. (2 minutes) The reflectors ask the presenter clarifying questions. Clarifying questions are for the person asking them. They ask the presenter who, what, where, when, and how. They are not "why" questions. The clarifying questions can be answered quickly and succinctly, often with just a phrase or two.

4. (30 seconds) Practice mindful breathing with your partner(s). It may be helpful to focus on the following phrases during the breathing periods:

Breathing in, I listen to my colleagues. Breathing out, I hear what they say. Breathing in, I seek to understand what students are learning. Breathing out, I look deeply at the data my colleague shares.

5. (2 minutes) Share data. Depending on the data being shared, this may take longer than 2 minutes. For example, if you are sharing a video of students performing an academic task or a student interview about the task, this could be longer.

6. (4 minutes) The reflectors talk with each other (not to the presenter) about the data and the inquiry focus. What did we hear? What didn't we hear that we think might be relevant? What did we notice about the data? What are we thinking now? The presenter does not speak during this discussion, but instead mindfully listens and takes notes.

(continued)

7. (2 minutes) The presenter responds to the discussion, sharing with the group anything that particularly resonated for them. The point of this time period is not for the presenter to give a detailed recap of the group's conversation. This is a time for the presenter to talk about the most significant comments, ideas, and questions heard and what they are now thinking in terms of new thoughts or questions that emerged while listening to the reflectors or potential shifts they'd like to now make to their teaching practice.

8. (90 seconds) Debrief how the mindful consultancy process was, reflecting on what SEL skills you just used with each other.

SEL Inquiry Focus	Focal Student(s)	Data	Reflections	Shifts
Connection between SEL and academics:	Why did I choose this student?	What's my data source? What do the data reveal?	What am I thinking now? What have I learned from my colleagues?	What's my next step based on analyzing the data?

GOING DEEPER

In the October 2018 issue of Educational Leadership, *The Promise of Social-Emotional Learning*, Daniela Mantilla, of Mills Teachers Scholars, discusses in her article, "What's SEL got to do with it?" how collaborative inquiry can support educators in growing both the "mindsets and the instructional practices needed to attend to students' social-emotional learning."

Using Honest, Open Questions

As we share about what's happening in our classrooms, another great resource to help deepen our inquiry is the use of honest, open questions. Honest, open questions are one of the Circle of Trust Touchstones developed by the Center for Courage and Renewal. These are questions we can ask ourselves, or our colleagues and they can also be helpful in coaching conversations. Honest, open questions aren't about fixing or advising; they are questions that deepen reflection, help us connect with our inner truth, and rest on the fundamental belief in the innate capacity of the person answering the honest, open question. When asking an honest, open question our job is to awaken one's inner wisdom.

EXAMPLES OF HONEST, OPEN QUESTIONS

- What surprises you most about this situation?
- What are you most afraid of happening?
- What is the hardest part for you about this?
- If you could wave a magic wand, what would you make happen?
- When have you experienced something similar to this before?
- What pattern or belief do you believe you're acting out?
- What do you really want?
- What might you be avoiding in this situation?
- What kind of support would be helpful to you?
- What does it feel like when you imagine making a decision?
- What potential alternatives can you imagine?
- What are you most attached to keeping or afraid of losing?
- What is the voice in your head saying about this situation?
- What judgment do you have about yourself in this situation?
- How does this situation help define who you are?
- How might you look at this situation differently?
- How could this situation be serving you?
- How might you be helping to create this situation?
- What animal or movie character are you embodying in this situation?

- What chapter in a book would you name this situation?
- If you were a superhero, what superpower would serve you now?

(Millennium.org, 2018)

At the start of this chapter, Dr. Paris Priore-Kim named three conditions she felt were essential to engage in reflective practice: time, mind-set, and trust. Making our learning public requires us to embrace vulnerability, and in order for teachers to do that, leaders need to create a culture where it feels safe enough to critically examine practice.

SEL Learning Walks

In my work implementing SEL with teaching teams, one of the most powerful practices has been coconstructing an SEL learning walk tool based on the SEL practices the team hopes to implement, leading a learning walk where we visit each others' classrooms and use the coconstructed tool to gather data, facilitating a conversation on what we saw, and identifying next steps.

In order for this practice to be successful, teachers have to feel comfortable opening up their classrooms, which depends on the culture in your school. In *Open Your Door: Why We Need to See Each Other Teach*,

Jennifer Gonzalez writes, "And though we work together, we usually follow parallel, rather than intersecting lines. We rarely ever actually see each other teach. And it's a shame, because every time I've observed a colleague, my admiration for them has grown, and each time, I felt a little closer to them" (2017). In this article, Gonzalez beautifully outlines the benefits of experiencing each other's practice. This is a great resource to offer if your colleagues are not yet open to observing each other in action.

Here's an example of a learning walk tool that was coconstructed with a team of ninth grade teachers I work with based on the SEL practices they were prioritizing.

Classroom Instruction	Evidence
Teacher embeds SEL goals and/or skills in academic content.	
Teacher employs collaborative and interactive structures that enable students to deepen and practice SEL skills.	
Student talk exceeds teacher talk.	
Students are attentive and engaged (note: compliant doesn't mean students are engaged).	

Classroom Instruction	Evidence
Teacher incorporated the three signature SEL practices.	
Students respectfully listen and talk with each other; question each other; agree or disagree; extend each other's thinking.	

When the actual learning walks took place, we used this agenda I developed to guide our time together. You can modify based on your context.

Learning Walk Agenda

Time	Activity
2 min	Welcoming ritual: What are you looking forward to around engaging in this SEL learning walk?

40 min
 	
(10 min in 4 classrooms back to back)
	• Capture evidence using the SEL learning walk tool
	• Focus on low-inference observations (facts without judgment)
	• As you walk, discuss and take notes on the following questions:
	  • What do you see?
	  • What don't you see?
	  • What do you hear?
	  • What conversations are happening?
	  • What do you wonder about?

Time	Activity
10 min	Short debrief: 1. What do you see? 2. What don't you see? 3. What do you hear? 4. What conversations are happening? 5. What do you wonder about?
2 min	Optimistic close: What's one takeaway from this experience?

Soon after the learning walk, we engaged in a fuller debrief with the teaching team, using the following agenda:

Time	Activity
5 min	Welcoming ritual: What are the benefits of observing peers in action?
35 min	1. Share what was observed and chart evidence. Try to make descriptive statements about what you saw and heard and avoid statements of judgment. 2. What does the data tell us? 3. What wonderings do you have as a result of the observations? How does what we observed further inform our understanding of SEL implementation and future SEL focus areas in our implementation? 4. Determine next steps.
5 min	Optimistic close: What's one positive surprise that you experienced during the SEL learning walk?

There are many SEL learning walk resources in development. For example, the Metropolitan Nashville Public School District has created a comprehensive schoolwide SEL walk-through rubric that focuses on three areas: (1) the school-wide environment; (2) classroom instruction; and (3) classroom environment, management, and discipline.

Feedback Protocol for SEL Integrated Lesson Plan

Sharing SEL integrated lesson plans with colleagues and receiving feedback is a great way to collectively prioritize SEL in academic instruction and grow collective responsibility around SEL at school sites.

This protocol can also be adapted for use in receiving feedback on unit plans by doubling the time for each activity, so each person shares and receives feedback for 30 minutes. In the initial sharing, presenting teachers speak to the suggested items in relation to the unit as a whole (e.g., SEL teaching practices used throughout the unit, unit goals inclusive of SEL goals, etc.).

Include a final debrief after every colleague has shared, focused on the following questions: *How did the feedback process go? What adjustments should be made to the protocol when it's used next time? What SEL skills did we use during our feedback protocol? How do you now feel about your connection to your colleagues compared to before you engaged in this protocol?*

Gather in Trios

Fifteen minutes each, three rounds: 45 minutes total.

Time	Activity
5 min	Teacher shares an overview of the lesson plan, paying special attention to: • Lesson goals inclusive of SEL goals • SEL teaching practices • How SEL shows up in the academic content and the learning process • How the teacher is planning to model SEL • Incorporation of the three signature SEL practices (welcoming ritual, engaging practices, optimistic closure)
2 min	Colleagues share what they appreciate about the design of the lesson and how they see it supporting SEL.
3 min	Colleagues ask questions to push presenting teacher's thinking, and teacher responds by thinking aloud. Example questions: How can you make SEL more explicit in your instruction? What are the ways in which you are incorporating student voice? How do you plan to address any challenges students may experience during the lesson? What might those challenges be?
2 min	Colleagues share any ideas, suggestions, and appreciations with the presenting teacher.
3 min	Presenting teacher shares what they are thinking now as a result of the collegial feedback and thanks their colleagues.

Measuring SEL

Assessing student SEL is a hot topic, and up until recently there weren't many tools for accurately assessing social and emotional competence. Using data to inform your SEL integrated efforts can strengthen your work, and even if your school isn't yet using an SEL-specific assessment, you can engage with attendance and discipline data as a starting point. Some states have surveys like the California Healthy Kids Survey, which is a comprehensive data system to assess the needs of the whole child. CASEL has also created the Establishing Practical Social-Emotional Competence Assessments of Preschool to High School Students project to advance efforts toward creating scientifically sound SEL assessments. The American Institutes for Research has developed the Ready to Assess toolkit, a comprehensive, free resource that can aid school and district leaders in reflecting on and choosing assessments on SEL. Panorama Education has also developed a free guide for district and school leaders on measuring SEL. Delving deep into assessment is beyond the scope of this publication, but I encourage you to read another SEL Solutions book, *Assessing Students' Social and Emotional Learning* by Clark McKown. This book can help you understand various types of SEL assessments (direct assessments, rating scales, self-report questionnaires, and structured observational systems) and decide how best to approach SEL assessment given your context.

Note From the Field

A great way to involve and empower students is to eventually have them participate in the SEL learning walk process by leading SEL walk-throughs. At one of the schools I worked at, I trained student leaders to lead and facilitate classroom observations focused on SEL.

What are some ways you could incorporate student voice into the SEL learning walk process?

Starting Where You Are

While several resources have been offered in this chapter to support reflective practice, one of the most important first steps we can take is to hold a stance of curiosity toward our work. Marc Brackett, founding director of the Yale Center for Emotional Intelligence, often talks about the importance of "being a scientist, not a judge." This statement can hold true in many aspects of our lives, such as holding a stance of curiosity and nonjudgment towards ourselves, others, and, professionally speaking, our own teaching practice. Take a moment to reflect on how you can apply "being a scientist, not a judge" to your teaching practice and choose one new idea from this chapter to apply.

Afterword

What's Love Got to Do With It?

Love is at the root of everything, all learning, all relationships, love or the lack of it.
—Fred Rogers

After giving birth to my son, Kailash, in the spring of 2018, I was in a heightened state in which I became radically more aware of the importance of human relationships. Emerging from my cocoon, I was lucky that the first film I went out to see as a new mother was *Won't You Be My Neighbor* (Neville, 2018), which explores the life and contributions of the host of the popular PBS children's program *Mister Rogers' Neighborhood*. For many of us, Rogers demonstrates what being a great teacher is all about. After seeing this inspiring movie, I realized that long before we had the term "social and emotional learning," Fred Rogers was teaching SEL and reinforcing in each episode that our sense of connection affects how we learn. Through his television program, he was in fact sharing the message that the network of human relationships we live in—let's call it love—is the fabric of our lives.

Love is a word we shy away from far too much in education. We need to be bold enough and brave enough to see it as central to our work as educators. If teaching and learning rest on the power of our relationships, then love is a critical element. A student's sense of belonging impacts academic performance and overall well-being, reminding us that young people often don't care how much you know, but care how much you care. SEL strategies are beneficial, but if the teachers employing these strategies aren't coming from a place of love, then they will ultimately be futile.

College and career readiness is an important goal to hold up for our students, and no doubt SEL contributes greatly toward the achievement of that goal, but I don't believe it should be our only North Star. The ultimate goal of SEL and our work as educators should be love—to create a classroom environment in which we and our students feel seen, safe, free, appreciated, and loved. I was recently listening to my favorite podcast, *On Being* with Krista Tippett, in which Tippett was interviewing my home state senator, Corey Booker. In the interview Senator Booker (2018) shared, "I believe in a radical love. I believe that we should love those who hate us. I believe we should love those who scorn us. Our nation right now is settling for this ideal of 'tolerance' when we should be reaching for the ideal of love. Tolerance is 'I'm stomaching your right to be different, but if you disappear off the face of the earth, I don't care—I'm no worse, I'm no better off.' Love says, 'I *see* you.'" When I think about my baby boy, what I most want for him in this life is to be seen and to see others—to experience and offer love on a daily basis. May all children we teach gain this sense of being seen.

Teachers are the engine that drives SEL programs and practices in schools, and their own social-emotional competence and well-being strongly influences their students.
—Dr. Kimberly Schonert-Reichl,
Professor of Human Development, University of British Columbia

Knowing how hectic, fast-paced, and busy the lives of teachers are, when I first set out to write this book, I planned to create the CliffsNotes for integrating SEL into instruction in secondary classrooms. What I realized through the process of writing this book is that while there are quick and easy ways to include SEL in our day-to-day classroom practice, there are no shortcuts to the emotional resonance of this work. Research continually confirms that the most integral factor in student acquisition of SEL is a teacher's own SEL. By allowing time and energy for our own self-reflection, self-compassion, and self-love, we nourish our ability to be truly great teachers. As James Baldwin said, "Children have never been very good at listening to their elders, but they have never failed to imitate them." We as educators must do our own work and cultivate love in ourselves and love for others to nourish our sense of interconnectedness for our own and our students' sake.

Recommended Resources

SEL and Equity

Pursuing Social and Emotional Development Through a Racial Equity Lens: A Call to Action & Pursuing Social and Emotional Development Through a Racial Equity Lens: 5 Strategies for System Leaders to Take Action (https://www.aspeninstitute.org/publications/pursuing-social-and-emotional -development-through-a-racial-equity-lens-a-call-to-action/)

Social-Emotional Learning & Equity Pitfalls and Recommendations (http://nationalequityproject.org/wp-content/uploads/social-emotional-learning -pitfalls-recs.pdf)

SEL and Culturally Responsive Teaching

Center for Reaching & Teaching the Whole Child (http://crtwc.org/)
Hammond, Z. (2015). *Culturally responsive teaching and the brain: Promoting authentic*

engagement and rigor among culturally and linguistically diverse students. Thousand Oaks, CA: Corwin, a SAGE Company.

Mindfulness

Aguilar, E. (2018). *Onward: Cultivating emotional resilience in educators.* San Francisco, CA: Jossey-Bass.

Broderick, Trish. (2019). *Mindfulness in the secondary classroom.* New York: Norton.

Cannon, J. (2016). Education as the Practice of Freedom: A Social Justice Proposal for Mindfulness Educators. *Mindfulness in Behavioral Health Handbook of Mindfulness,* 397-409. doi:10.1007/978-3-319-44019-4_26

CARE for Teachers (http://www.care4teachers.com/)

Hawkins, Kevin. (2017). *Mindful teacher, mindful school: improving well-being in teaching and learning.* Los Angeles: Sage.

Jennings, Patricia J. (2015). *Mindfulness for teachers: Simple skills for peace and productivity in the classroom.* New York: Norton.

Lantieri, L., & Zakrzewski, V. (2015, April 15). How SEL and mindfulness can work together. *Greater Good Magazine.* https://greatergood.berkeley.edu/article/item/how_social_emotional_learning_and_mindfulness_can_work_together

Mason, Christine, Murphy, Michele Rivers, & Jackson, Yvette. (2018). *Mindfulness practices: Cultivating heart-centered school communities where students focus and flourish.* Bloomington, IN: Solution Tree.

Mindful Schools (https://www.mindfulschools.org)

Mindful Education Online Training (https://mindfuleducation.com/)

Nhất Hạnh, Thich, & Weare, Katherine. (2017). *Happy teachers change the world: A guide for cultivating mindfulness in education.* Berkeley, CA: Parallax Press.

Rechtschaffen, Daniel. (2014). *The way of mindful education: Cultivating well-being in teachers and students.* New York: Norton.

Srinivasan, Meena. (2014). *Teach, breathe, learn: Mindfulness in and out of the classroom.* Berkeley, CA: Parallax Press.

Restorative Practices

Boyes-Watson, Carolyn, & Kay Pranis. (2014). *Circle forward: Building a restorative school community*. St. Paul, MN: Living Justice.

Engaging Schools (previously known as Educators for Social Responsibility, ESR) (http://engagingschools.org/)

International Institute for Restorative Practices (https://www.iirp.edu/)

Morningside Center for Teaching Social Responsibility (http://www.morningsidecenter.org/)

Restorative Justice Training Institute (http://www.rjtica.org/)

Three Signature SEL Practices

Frazier, Nicole, & Donna Mehle. (2013). *Activators: Classroom strategies for engaging students in middle and high school*. Cambridge, MA: Educators for Social Responsibility.

Kuczala, M., & Lengel, T. (2017). *Ready, set, go! The Kinesthetic Classroom 2.0*. Thousand Oaks, CA: Corwin.

Liberating Structures (http://www.liberatingstructures.com/ls/)

SEL Teaching Practices

Buck Institute for Education, Project-Based Learning (http://www.bie.org/)

EL Education, Collaborative Culture: Protocols (https://eleducation.org/resources/collaborative-culture-protocols)

Engaging Schools, Multiday Institutes (http://engagingschools.org/workshops-and-institutes/institutes/)

Johnson, D. W., Johnson, R. T., & Holubec, E. J. (2009). *Circles of learning: Cooperation in the classroom*. Edina, MN: Interaction.

Kagan Publishing and Professional Development (https://www.kaganonline.com/)

Yoder, Nick. (2014). Teaching the whole child: Instructional practices that support social-emotional learning in three teacher evaluation frameworks. Washington, DC: American Institutes for Research.

Zwiers, J., & Crawford, M. (2011). *Academic conversations: Classroom talk that fosters critical thinking and content understandings.* Portland, ME: Stenhouse.

SEL Integrated Lesson Planning

Elias, M. J., & Tobias, S. E. (2018). *Boost emotional intelligence in students: 30 flexible research-based activities to build EQ skills (grades 5–9).* Minneapolis: Free Spirit.

Wiggins, G. P., & McTighe, J. (2008). *Understanding by design.* Alexandria, VA: Association for Supervision and Curriculum Development.

Measuring SEL

American Institutes for Research, Ready to Assess SEL Toolkit (https://www.air.org/resource/are-you-ready-assess-social-and-emotional-development)

McKown, Clark. *Assessing students' social and emotional learning.* . (Norton, 2019).

Measuring SEL (https://measuringsel.casel.org/)

Panorama Education. *Measure and understand social-emotional learning.* (https://www.panoramaed.com/social-emotional-learning)

Reflective Practice

Hall, Pete, & Simeral, Alisa. (2017). *Creating a culture of reflective practice: Capacity-building for schoolwide success.* Alexandria, VA: ASCD.

Mantilla, D. (2018, October). Collaborative Inquiry: What's SEL Got to Do with It? Retrieved from http://www.ascd.org/publications/educational-leadership/oct18/vol76/num02/What's-SEL-Got-to-Do-with-It%C2%A2.aspx

Schon, Donald. (1983). *The reflective practitioner: How professionals think in action.* New York: Basic Books.

Shagoury, Ruth, & Power, Brenda Miller. (2003). *The art of classroom inquiry.* New York: Heinemann.

References

Abel, N. (2016, February 16). What is personalized learning? iNACOL. Retrieved from https://www.inacol.org/news/what-is-personalized-learning/

AIR. (2015, December 15). Are you ready to assess social and emotional development? American Institutes for Research. Retrieved from https://www.air.org/resource/are-you-ready-assess-social-and-emotional-development

Alliance for Excellent Education. (2014, July 17). Teacher attrition costs United States up to $2.2 billion annually, says new Alliance report. Retrieved from https://all4ed.org/press/teacher-attrition-costs-united-states-up-to-2-2-billion-annually-says-new-alliance-report/

Atwell, M. N., Bridgeland, J. M., DePaoli, J. L., & Shriver, T. P. (November, 2018). *Respected:Perspectives of Youth on High School & Social and Emotional Learning*, A Report for CASEL by Civic with Hart Research Associates.

Aspen Institute. (2018, May). Pursuing social and emotional development through a racial equity lens: A call to action (Issue brief). Retrieved from https://assets.aspeninstitute.org/content/uploads/2018/05/Aspen-Institute_Framing-Doc_Call-to-Action.pdf

Bandura, A. (1986). *Social foundations of thought and action: A social cognitive theory.* Englewood Cliffs, NJ: Prentice-Hall.

Bennett, C. (2016, March 6). Wait time is think time in the secondary classroom. ThoughtCo.

Berman, S., Chaffee, S., & Sarmiento, J. (2018, May). *The practice base for how we learn: Supporting students' social, emotional, and academic development.* National Commission on Social, Emotional, and Academic Development, Aspen Institute. doi:https://assets.aspeninstitute.org/content/uploads/2018/03/CDE-Practice -Base_FINAL.pdf

Booker, C. (2018, July 26). Civic spiritual evolution. Retrieved from https://onbeing .org/programs/cory-booker-civic-spiritual-evolution-jul2018/

Boyes-Watson, C., & Pranis, K. (2014). *Circle forward.* St. Paul, MN: Living Justice.

Brinson, D., & Steiner, L. (2007). *Building collective efficacy: How leaders inspire teachers to achieve* (issue brief). Washington, DC: Center for Comprehensive School Reform and Improvement. doi:https://files.eric.ed.gov/fulltext/ED499254.pdf

Buck Institute for Education. (2009, September 28). High school project: Save the beach. Retrieved from https://www.youtube.com/watch?v=cJ5Z53JAivE

Cannon, J. (2016). Education as the Practice of Freedom: A Social Justice Proposal for Mindfulness Educators. *Mindfulness in Behavioral Health Handbook of Mindfulness,* 397-409. doi:10.1007/978-3-319-44019-4_26

CASEL. (2015). *2015 CASEL guide: Effective social and emotional learning programs— middle and high school edition.* Retrieved from https://www.casel.org/middle-and -high-school-edition-casel-guide/

CASEL. (2018, February). *Leveraging SEL to promote equity: What educators need to know and do* [video webinar]. Retrieved from https://casel.org/wp-content/ uploads/2018/02/Equity-SEL-webinar.pdf

CDC. (2014). Youth risk behavior surveillance: United States, 2013. *Morbidity and Mortality Weekly Report, 63*(4). Retrieved from https://www.cdc.gov/mmwr/pdf/ ss/ss6304.pdf

Chatmon, L. R., & Osta, K. (2018, August 20). 5 steps for liberating public education from its deep racial bias. *Education Week.* Retrieved from https://www.edweek .org/ew/articles/2018/08/22/5-steps-for-liberating-public-education-from.html

City, E. (2011, October). Learning from instructional rounds. *Educational Leadership,* 36–41.

Civic Enterprises, Bridgeland, J., Bruce, M., & Hariharan. (2013). *The missing piece:*

A national teacher survey on how social and emotional learning can empower children and transform schools. Retrieved from https://casel.org/the-missing-piece-a -national-teacher-survey-on-how-social-and-emotional-learning-can-empower -children-and-transform-schools/

Cody, A. (2011, October 12). Improving Teaching 101: Teacher action research. Retrieved from http://blogs.edweek.org/teachers/living-in-dialogue/2011/10/ improving_teaching_101_collabo.html

Common Core State Standards Initiative. (n.d.). College and career readiness anchor standards for speaking and listening. Retrieved from http://www.corestandards .org/ELA-Literacy/CCRA/SL/

Conley, D. T. (2018, February 28). Rethinking the notion of "noncognitive." Retrieved from https://www.edweek.org/ew/articles/2013/01/23/18conley.h32.html

Council of the Great City Schools. (2010, fall). Urban school superintendents: Characteristics, tenure, and salary, seventh survey and report. *Urban Indicator.* Retrieved from doi:https://www.cgcs.org/cms/lib/DC00001581/Centricity/ Domain/4/Supt_Survey2010.pdf

Covey, S. R. (1989). *The seven habits of highly effective people.* New York: Simon and Schuster.

Davidson, R. (2008, February 27). The heart-brain connection: The neuroscience of social, emotional, and academic learning. Retrieved from https://www .edutopia.org/video/heart-brain-connection-neuroscience-social-emotional -and-academic-learning

Davidson, R. J. (2015). Behavioral Interventions Produce Robust Beneficial Biological Alterations. *Biological Psychiatry, 78*(10), 668–669. doi:10.1016/j. biopsych.2015.09.001

Dean, C. B., Hubbell, E. R., Pitler, H., Stone, B. J., & Marzano, R. J. (2012). *Classroom instruction that works: Research-based strategies for increasing student achievement.* Alexandria, VA: ASCD.

DeBerard, M. Scott, Glen I. Spielmans, & Deana C. Julka. "Predictors Of Academic Achievement And Retention Among College Freshmen: A Longitudinal Study." College Student Journal 38.1 (2004): 66–80. Academic Search Premier. Web. 20 Apr. 2012.

Durlak, J. A., Weissberg, R. P., Dymnicki, A. B., Taylor, R. D., & Schellinger, K.

(2011). The impact of enhancing students' social and emotional learning: A meta-analysis of school-based universal interventions. *Child Development, 82,* 405–432.

Dusenbury, L., Sarley, D., Weissberg, R. P., & Domitrovich, C. E. (2016). *Eight key components of mindful awareness practices (MAPs) identified through the lens of best practice and research in social and emotional learning (SEL): A collaborative paper by the Collaborative for Academic, Social, and Emotional Learning (CASEL) and the 1440 Foundation.*

Dusenbury, L., & Weissberg, R. P. (2018). *Emerging insights from states' efforts to strengthen social and emotional learning.* Chicago: CASEL. doi:https://casel.org/wp-content/uploads/2018/06/CSI-Insights.pdf

Dymnicki, A., Sambolt, M., & Kidron, Y. (2013). *Improving college and career readiness by incorporating social and emotional learning.* Washington, DC: American Institutes for Research College and Career Readiness and Success Center.

EdWords. (n.d.). What is student agency? Retrieved from https://www.renaissance.com/edwords/student-agency/

Elias, M. (2018, July 4). Emotional intelligence: Why should we teach it. Retrieved from https://www.middleweb.com/38066/emotional-intelligence-and-why-should-we-teach-it/

Elmore, R. (1999, winter). Building a new structure for school leadership. *American Educator.*

Eva, A. L., & Thayer, N. M. (2016, October 17). "The mindful teacher: Translating research into daily well-being." *Clearing House, 90*(1): 18–25. doi:10.1080/00098655.2016.1235953

Farrell, T. S. (2014, November). "Teacher you are stupid!" Cultivating a reflective disposition. *Electronic Journal for English as a Second Language, 18*(3). Retrieved from http://www.tesl-ej.org/wordpress/issues/volume18/ej71/ej71a2/

Farrington, C., Roderick, M., Allensworth, E., Nagaoak, J., Keyes, T. S., Johnson, D. W., & Beechum, N. O. (2012). *Teaching adolescents to become learners: The role of noncognitive factors in shaping school performance: A critical literature review.* Chicago: University of Chicago Consortium on Chicago School Research. doi:https://consortium.uchicago.edu/sites/default/files/publications/Noncognitive Report.pdf

Fischer, K. (2013, March). The employment mismatch. *Chronicle of Higher Education.*

Flook, L., Goldberg, S. B., Pinger, L., Bonus, K., & Davidson, R. J. (2013). Mindfulness for teachers: A pilot study to assess effects on stress, burnout, and teaching efficacy. *Mind, Brain, and Education, 7*(3), 182–195. doi:10.1111/mbe.12026

Flook, L., Smalley, S., Kitil, M. J., Galla, B., Kaiser-Greenland, S., Locke, J., Ishijima, E., & Kasari, C. (2010). Effects of mindful awareness practices on executive functions in elementary school children. *Journal of Applied School Psychology, 26*(1), 70–95.

George Lucas Educational Foundation. (2018, August 10). 60-second strategy: Appreciation, apology, aha! Retrieved from https://www.edutopia.org/video/60-second-strategy-appreciation-apology-aha

Gonzalez, J. (2017, September 22). Why we need to see each other teach. Retrieved from https://www.cultofpedagogy.com/open-your-door/

Graeber, A. (2012, September 11). Practical PBL series: Design an instructional unit in seven phases. Retrieved from https://www.edutopia.org/blog/practical-pbl-design-amber-graeber

Great Schools Partnership. (2013, December 20). Student voice. Retrieved from https://www.edglossary.org/student-voice

Hagelskamp, C., Brackett, M. A., Rivers, S. E., & Salovey, P. (2013). Improving classroom quality with the RULER approach to social and emotional learning: Proximal and distal outcomes. *American Journal of Community Psychology, 51*(3–4), 530–543. doi:10.1007/s10464-013-9570-x

Hammond, Z. (2015). *Culturally responsive teaching and the brain: Promoting authentic engagement and rigor among culturally and linguistically diverse students.* Thousand Oaks, CA: Corwin, a SAGE Company.

Harvey, O.J., and Schroder, H.M. (1963). Cognitive aspects of self and motivation. In O. J. Harvey (Ed.), Motivation and social interaction-cognitive determinants. (pp. 95–133). New York: Ronald Press.

Hattie, J. (2012). *Visible learning for teachers: Maximizing impact on learning.* New York: Routledge.

Hoffeld, D. (2017, February 24). Want to know what your brain does when it hears a question? Retrieved from https://www.fastcompany.com/3068341/want-to-know-what-your-brain-does-when-it-hears-a-question_*In Support of How We*

Learn: A Youth Call to Action. (2018). Aspen Institute Youth Commission on Social, Emotional, and Academic Development.

Jagers, R. J., Rivas-Drake, D., & Borowski, T. (November, 2018). *Measuring SEL, Using Data to Inspire Practice: Equity & Social and Emotional Learning: A Cultural Analysis.* Establishing Practical Social-Emotional Competence Assessments Work Group, CASEL. doi:https://measuringsel.casel.org/wp-content/uploads/2018/11/Frameworks-Equity.pdf

Jain, S., Bassey, H., Brown, M., & Kalra, P. (2014, September). *Restorative justice in Oakland schools, implementation and impacts: An effective strategy to reduce racially disproportionate discipline, suspensions and improve academic outcomes.* Retrieved from https://www.ousd.org/cms/lib/CA01001176/Centricity/Domain/134/OUSD-RJ%20Report%20revised%20Final.pdf

Jennings, P. A., Brown, J. L., Frank, J. L., Doyle, S., Oh, Y., Davis, R., . . . Greenberg, M. T. (2017, February 13). Impacts of the CARE for Teachers Program on teachers' social and emotional competence and classroom interactions. *Journal of Educational Psychology.* http://dx.doi.org/10.1037/edu0000187

Johnson, H., & Wiener, R. (2017). This time, with feeling: Integrating social and emotional development and college- and career-readiness standards (issue brief). doi:https://assets.aspeninstitute.org/content/uploads/2017/05/ThisTimeWithFeeling.pdf

Jones, S. M., Bouffard, S. M., & Weissbourd, R. (2013, May 1). Educators' social and emotional skills vital to learning: Social and emotional competencies aren't secondary to the mission of education, but are concrete factors in the success of teachers, students, and schools. *Phi Delta Kappan.*

Jones, S., & Kahn, J. (2017, September). The evidence base for how we learn: Supporting students' social, emotional, and academic development. National Commission on Social, Emotional, and Academic Development. doi:https://assets.aspeninstitute.org/content/uploads/2018/03/FINAL_CDS-Evidence-Base.pdf

Kagan, S. (2011, fall/winter). The "P" and "I" of PIES: Powerful principles for success. *Kagan Online Magazine.*

Kemeny, M. E., Foltz, C., Cavanagh, J. F., Cullen, M., Giese-Davis, J., Jennings, P., . . . Allen, J. P. (2012). Teacher-student relationships and engagement: Conceptualizing, measuring, and improving the capacity of classroom interactions. In S. Christenson, A. Reschly, & C. Wylie (Eds.), *Handbook of research on stu-*

dent engagement. Boston: Springer. Retrieved from https://link.springer.com/chapter/10.1007/978-1-4614-2018-7_17

Knight, S. (2015, December 11). Building social-emotional learning skills through cooperative learning. Retrieved from http://inservice.ascd.org/building-social-emotional-learning-skills-through-cooperative-learning/

Lantieri, L., & Zakrzewski, V. (2015, April 15). How SEL and mindfulness can work together. *Greater Good Magazine.* https://greatergood.berkeley.edu/article/item/how_social_emotional_learning_and_mindfulness_can_work_together

M., J. (2016, September 7). Teachers are master multi-taskers (but we already knew that . . .). Retrieved from https://everydayteacherstyle.com/2016/09/teachers-are-master-multi-taskers-but-we-already-knew-that/

Mantilla, D. (2018, October). Collaborative Inquiry: Whats SEL Got to Do with It? Retrieved from http://www.ascd.org/publications/educational-leadership/oct18/vol76/num02/What's-SEL-Got-to-Do-with-It%C2%A2.aspx

Marzano, R. J., Pickering, D., & Heflebower, T. (2011). *The highly engaged classroom.* Bloomington, IN: Marzano Research.

Moss, C. M., Brookhart, S. M., & Long, B. A. (2011, March). Knowing your learning target. *Educational Leadership, 68*(6), 66–69. doi:http://www.ascd.org/publications/educational-leadership/mar11/vol68/num06/knowing-your-learning-target.aspx

Mueller, C. M., & Dweck, C. S. (1998). Praise for intelligence can undermine children's motivation and performance. *Journal of Personality and Social Psychology, 75*(1), 33–52. http://dx.doi.org/10.1037/0022-3514.75.1.33

National Center for Education Statistics. (n.d.). Graduation rates. Retrieved from https://nces.ed.gov/fastfacts/display.asp?id=40

Neville, M. (Director). (2018). *Won't you be my neighbor.* Focus Features.

NSCC. (2007). The school climate challenge: Narrowing the gap between school climate research and school climate policy, practice guidelines and teacher education policy (White paper). Retrieved from doi:https://www.schoolclimate.org/themes/schoolclimate/assets/pdf/policy/school-climate-challenge-web.pdf

Offermann, L., & Rosh, L. (2012, June 13). Building trust through skillful self-disclosure. *Harvard Business Review.* Retrieved from https://hbr.org/2012/06/instantaneous-intimacy-skillfu

Oyserman, D., Bybee, D., and Terry, K. (2006). Possible selves and academic outcomes: How and when possible selves impel action. *Journal of Personality and Social Psychology,* 91, 188–204.

Parker, J. (2018, May 04). The Four Components of an Equitable Classroom. Retrieved from https://blogs.edweek.org/teachers/everyday_equity/2018/05/four_cs_of_an_equitable_c.html

Pianta, R. C., Hamre, B. K., & Allen, J. P. (2012). Teacher-Student Relationships and Engagement: Conceptualizing, Measuring, and Improving the Capacity of Classroom Interactions. *Handbook of Research on Student Engagement,* 365-386. doi:10.1007/978-1-4614-2018-7_17

Roeser, R. W., Schonert-Reichl, K. A., Jha, A., Cullen, M., Wallace, L., Wilensky, R., . . . Harrison, J. (2013, April 29). Mindfulness training and reductions in teacher stress and burnout: Results from two randomized, waitlist-control field trials. *Journal of Educational Psychology,* 105(3), 787–804. doi:10.1037/a0032093

Roeser, R. W., Skinner, E., Beers, J., & Jennings, P.A. (2012). Mindfulness training and teachers' professional development: An emerging area of research and practice. *Child Development Perspectives,* 6(2): 167–173. doi:10.1111/j.1750-8606.2012.00238.x

Rosales, J. (2017, June 30). How ESSA helps advance social and emotional learning. Retrieved from http://neatoday.org/2017/06/30/essa-sel/

Rose, M. (20138 January 15). Giving cognition a bad name. *Education Week.* Retrieved from https://www.edweek.org/ew/articles/2013/01/16/17rose_ep.h32.html

Rosenberg, E. L., Gillath, O., Shaver, P. R., Wallace, B. A., & Ekman, P. (2012). Contemplative/emotion training reduces negative emotional behavior and promotes prosocial responses. *Emotion,* 12(2): 338–350. doi: 10.1037/a0026118

RWJF. (2015, July 16). Children with strong social skills in kindergarten more likely to thrive as adults. Retrieved from https://www.rwjf.org/en/library/articles-and-news/2015/07/new-research--children-with-strong-social-skills-in-kindergarten.html

Sacks, A. (2017, May 8). The birth of a mother. *New York Times.* Retrieved from https://www.nytimes.com/2017/05/08/well/family/the-birth-of-a-mother.html

Schafler, K. (2017, November 14). How to change your life in one second flat. Retrieved from https://www.thriveglobal.com/stories/16020-4-questions-we-unconsciously-ask-near-constantly

Shafer, L. (2016, July 15). What makes SEL work? Retrieved from https://www.gse .harvard.edu/news/uk/16/07/what-makes-sel-work

Spinks, S. (Director). (2002). *Inside the teenage brain* [Video]. *Frontline*, PBS. Retrieved from https://www.pbs.org/wgbh/pages/frontline/shows/teenbrain/

Srinivasan, M. (2014). *Teach, breathe, learn: Mindfulness in and out of the classroom.* Berkeley, CA: Parallax.

Timperley, H., Kaser, L., & Halbert, J. (2014, April). A framework for transforming learning in schools: Innovation and the spiral of inquiry. Centre for Strategic Education Seminar Series Paper No. 234. Retrieved from https://educationcouncil .org.nz/sites/default/files/49.%20Spiral%20of%20Inquiry%20Paper%20-%20 Timperley%20Kaser%20Halbert.pdf

Wagenheim, J. (2016, winter). There's nothing soft about these skills. *Harvard Ed. Magazine.* Retrieved from https://www.gse.harvard.edu/news/ed/16/01/theres -nothing-soft-about-these-skills

Wiggins, G. P., & McTighe, J. (2008). *Understanding by design.* Alexandria, VA: Association for Supervision and Curriculum Development.

Yeager, D. S. (2017, spring). Social-emotional learning programs for adolescents. *Future of Children, Princeton-Brookings, 27*(1): 31–52.

Yoder, Nick. (2014). Teaching the whole child: Instructional practices that support social-emotional learning in three teacher evaluation frameworks. Washington, DC: American Institutes for Research.

Zwiers, J., & Crawford, M. (2011). *Academic conversations: Classroom talk that fosters critical thinking and content understandings.* Portland, ME: Stenhouse.

Index

Note: Italicized page locators refer to figures; tables are noted with a *t*.

About the Author

Meena Srinivasan, M.A., National Board Certified Teacher, is the Executive Director of Transformative Educational Leadership (TEL) an empowering, racially and culturally diverse, compassion-centered, innovative program for educational leaders who are called to integrate mindfulness-based social, emotional, academic and ethical learning into schools and school systems (www. teleadership.org). She has been teaching and leading with an equity focus in the fields of Social and Emotional Learning (SEL) and Mindful Awareness Practices (MAP) for over 16 years and has taught and worked in a variety of school settings—public, private, and international. She spent five and a half years working in partnership with the Collaborative for Academic, Social and Emotional Learning (CASEL) to implement SEL system-wide in the Oakland Unified School District, is a National Board Certified Teacher and holds a Clear Administrative Services Credential in the state of California. Meena is also a student of the late Ramchandra Gandhi (Mahatma Gandhi's grandson) and Nobel

Peace Prize Nominee, Thich Nhat Hanh. She was a contributor to Thich Nhat Hanh's bestselling books *Planting Seeds: Practicing Mindfulness with Children* and *Happy Teachers Change the World: A Guide for Cultivating Mindfulness in Education*. Meena's first book, *Teach, Breathe, Learn: Mindfulness in and out of the Classroom* (Parallax Press, 2014) was featured on Edutopia. She's a Registered Yoga Teacher, served on the Board of Directors of the Mindfulness in Education Network, was Core Faculty of the Mindful Education Institute, and served on the Advisory Board of the San Francisco Asian Art Museum's exhibit, Yoga: The Art of Transformation, the first major exhibition to explore yoga. Meena spent five years living in India studying contemplative practices while teaching at the American Embassy School and bringing mindfulness to educators and children across the region through Thich Nhat Hanh's India based non-profit Ahimsa Trust. Meena also trained in teaching Mindfulness Based Stress Reduction (MBSR) at UMASS Medical School's Stress Reduction Clinic and is a recipient of the Hemera Foundation Contemplative Education Fellowship. Outside of the education world she has worked in the fields of journalism and public policy and had a variety of professional experiences at organizations including: ABC Network News, Reuters, Bloomberg, the Woodrow Wilson International Center for Scholars, and the International Bureau of Education. A contributor to United Nations publications on inclusive education, Meena earned a Master's degree in Education from UC Berkeley and a Bachelor's degree in History and Political Science from Amherst College. Her international outlook was enhanced by spending her junior year studying abroad at the London School of Economics. Meena lives in the San Francisco Bay Area with her husband, Eurasian-American, Emmy-nominated filmmaker, Chihiro Wimbush, and her son, Kailash Sora Wimbush. Learn more at meenasrinivasan.com.